. No. ....

abh

(Mea

peri

e of

of the CORDON BLEU

TECHNIQUES AND RECIPES
VEGETABLES
& SALADS

LE CORDON BLEU

TECHNIQUES AND RECIPES

VEGETABLES
& SALADS

JENI WRIGHT AND ERIC TREUILLE

CASSELL

A CASSELL BOOK

This edition first published in the United Kingdom in 1998 by
Cassell plc
Wellington House
125 Strand
London WC2R 0BB

Created and Produced by
CARROLL & BROWN LIMITED
20 Lonsdale Road
London NW6 6RD

Material in this book has been previously published in
Le Cordon Bleu Complete Cooking Techniques
published by Cassell at £25

British Library Catalogue-in-Publication Data
A catalogue record for this book is available from the
British Library

ISBN 0-304-35123-7

Reproduced by Colourscan, Singapore
Printed and bound in Great Britain by Jarrold Book Printing,
Thetford, Norfolk

CONTENTS

CHOOSING VEGETABLES

Choose vegetables in season when they are at their freshest and most readily available; this is when they will taste their best and be at their most nutritious. Always look for crisp, fresh looking vegetables that have brightly coloured leaves. Avoid any that have brown patches, wilted leaves, bruised or pulpy flesh.

CARROTS should have fresh looking, healthy leafy tops, not discoloured or wilting

ONIONS should have dry papery skins; red onions should have no brown discoloration

POTATOES should be firm and well shaped with no "eyes" or green patches

TOMATO SKIN should be smooth and firm with no cuts or blemishes

ROOTS & TUBERS

Carrots, potatoes, beetroots, swedes, celeriac and radishes should have firm, heavy flesh and wrinkle-free skin. Avoid soft patches or sprouting.

MUSHROOMS

Choose firm, fresh looking mushrooms that have a soft "bloom" and fresh smell. The stalk end should be moist; if dry they may be slightly old.

ONIONS

Choose firm bulbs with even-coloured skins and no signs of sprouting. Avoid any that look damp or smell musty. Leeks and spring onions should have dark green leaves and fresh looking roots.

VEGETABLE FRUITS

Tomatoes, aubergines, peppers and avocados should have firm, smooth, shiny skins and a deep, even colour. Avoid any that are soft, pulpy or wrinkled.

SALAD LEAVES

Choose lettuces and cresses that smell fresh and look slightly damp on the surface. Check the heart is well formed. There should be no wilting or brown patches on the leaves.

LEAFY GREENS

Choose endive, Swiss chard and spinach with crisp, fresh looking greens. Leaves should feel springy to the touch; avoid any that appear limp or wilted. There should be no sign of insect damage.

STALKS & SHOOTS

Celery, globe artichokes, fennel, asparagus and chicory should have tightly packed, firm heads with no visible brown patches on outer layers.

ASPARAGUS should have plump stalks with tight buds, even in size and colour

LEAFY GREENS should have full, well formed head, crisp leaves with fresh green tips

PEAS should not have any visible dry or brown patches

SPINACH LEAVES are best when small and moist, with fine stalks

PODS & SEEDS

Select peas and beans with bright green pods that are full and plump. Choose sweetcorn with tight green husks and plump, even, shiny kernels. The kernels should be tightly packed on the cob.

BRASSICAS

Look for cauliflower, broccoli, Brussels sprouts and cabbage with undamaged tight compact heads. Outer leaves should be fresh with no signs of wilting or yellowing. Stalks should look moist and freshly cut.

BROCCOLI of the purple "hearting" variety should have dark coloured tightly formed florets, firm stalks, no signs of yellowing

BRASSICAS

This large family of vegetables includes cabbages, cauliflower, broccoli, and Brussels sprouts, as well as Oriental greens like mustard cabbage and *pak choi*.

SETTING THE COLOUR OF RED CABBAGE

Once cut, red cabbage has a tendency to turn blue or purple. This simple technique helps it keep its red colour.

1 Pour hot red wine vinegar over shredded cabbage (about 4 tbsp is enough for ½ small head of cabbage). Mix well and let stand for 5–10 minutes, then drain off excess vinegar.

2 Serve the red cabbage raw, tossed in a vinaigrette dressing and sprinkled with chopped parsley, or use in cooked dishes.

CORING CABBAGE

The hard white core at the centre of all cabbage is tough and inedible and should be removed to allow easy shredding and even cooking of the cabbage leaves.

Remove any outer, damaged leaves. Cut the cabbage lengthwise into quarters with a chef's knife. Cut off the base of each quarter at an angle to remove the hard white core. The cabbage is now ready to be shredded.

SHREDDING CABBAGE

After cutting a cabbage into quarters and coring it (see above), it can be shredded for eating raw in salads and coleslaws (see below), or for stir-frying, steaming or simmering in soups such as minestrone. Cabbage can be shredded either by hand or in a food processor.

BY HAND

Lay each cabbage quarter on a cutting board. Cut across to form even strips.

BY MACHINE

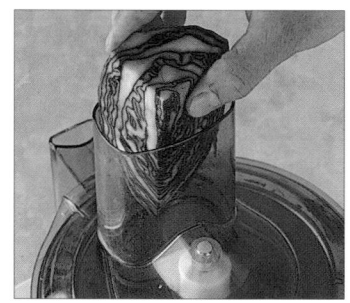

With the processor running, feed each cabbage quarter into the machine and shred.

COMBINING COLOURS

A colourful mixture of shredded red, white and green cabbage leaves looks very attractive and, with its mix of textures and flavours, makes an excellent winter salad.

Shred the cabbage either by hand or machine (see above) and place in a bowl. Toss in a vinaigrette or cooked dressing, or in mayonnaise.

PREPARING BROCCOLI AND CAULIFLOWER

The delicate florets and hard stalks of broccoli and cauliflower cook at different rates so you need to separate them before cooking. Broccoli is illustrated here.

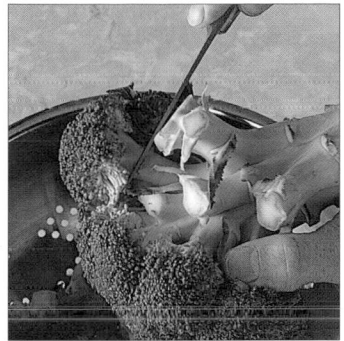

1 Holding the vegetable over a colander, cut off the florets leaving only the stalk. Divide the larger florets into smaller ones.

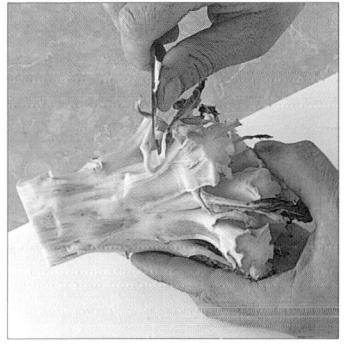

2 Remove the leaves from the stalk. Peel away the tough, outer layer with a vegetable peeler, then cut the stalk lengthwise in half.

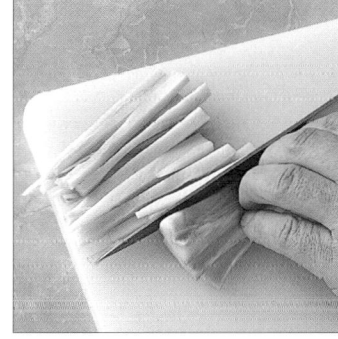

3 Put the stalk cut-side down and remove the ends. Cut the stalk lengthwise into slices; cut the slices lengthwise into sticks.

SUPERSTAR VEGETABLE

Brassicas are all good sources of vitamin C and minerals, but broccoli is particularly high in many vital nutrients.

- 100 g broccoli provides over half the recommended daily intake of vitamin C.
- Broccoli is rich in carotene. High intakes may provide protection against cancer and heart disease.
- Broccoli is rich in folate (folic acid) which is needed by the body to form DNA and process proteins.
- The minerals iron, potassium and chromium are found in significant amounts in broccoli.

PREPARING BRUSSELS SPROUTS

To ensure even cooking of large sprouts, a cross is cut in the base. This is not necessary for small sprouts.

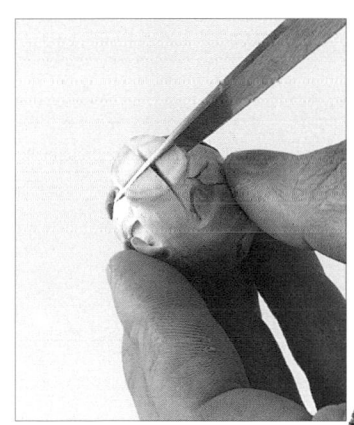

Cut a cross shape in the base of sprout with a chef's knife. Cut only a quarter of the way into the sprout, or it may fall apart during cooking. Trim the base stalks and remove any discoloured outer leaves.

TRICK OF THE TRADE

PREVENTING DISCOLORATION

White vegetables, such as the cauliflower shown here, have a tendency to discolour when cut and exposed to the air. To prevent discoloration, put the prepared vegetable in a bowl, cover with cold water and add 1 tbsp lemon juice or white wine vinegar. This acidulates the water and preserves the colour of the vegetable.

From left to right:
Broccoli; Brussels sprouts; Cauliflower

LEAFY GREENS

Although they are all prepared in much the same way, these greens run the gamut in flavour and texture. Young, tender varieties generally have a mild taste and can be eaten whole and raw. Large tougher-textured leaves need their stalks removed before cooking.

From the sweet and earthy to the sharp and peppery, greens have a wide variety of tastes. All require thorough rinsing to remove surface dirt before use.

CHINESE MUSTARD GREENS: With its strong, peppery bite, this green is best cooked; trim stalk before using.

FRENCH DANDELION: This jagged-leaved vegetable needs its tough root removed before use. Cultivated varieties have a milder taste than wild dandelions. Eat raw or cooked.

GRAPE LEAVES: These serve as a wrapper for other foods. Fresh leaves should be blanched, those sold in brine simply rinsed before use.

SORREL: Trim stalks of this tart, lemony green before eating raw or in cooked dishes.

SWISS CHARD: Separate the leaves from the white central stalks. Both leaves and stalks can be cooked.

PREPARING SPINACH

Young spinach leaves are tender so they can be eaten whole, either raw or cooked. Mature varieties have a tough stalk that needs trimming before the leaves are briefly cooked in just the water that clings to the leaves after washing. A technique that makes a stylish presentation for raw or gently sautéed spinach is the classic chiffonade *illustrated here.*

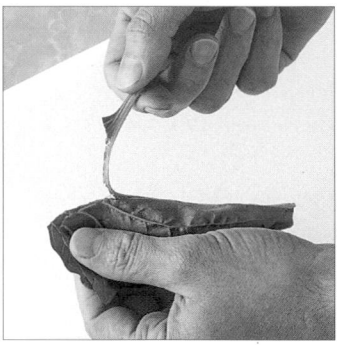
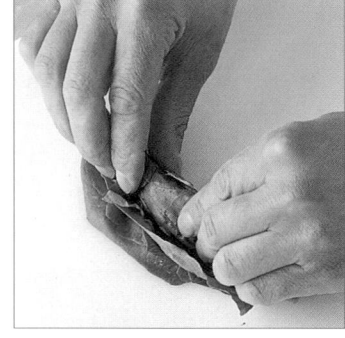

1 Fold each spinach leaf lengthwise along the central rib with the rib facing outwards. Tear the rib away from the leaf.

2 Stack a few leaves and roll them lengthwise into a cylindrical bundle. Hold the bundle with one hand.

3 Cut across the bundle with a chef's knife, using your knuckles as a guide, to make thin strips.

From left to right: sorrel; Chinese mustard greens; Swiss chard; French dandelion; spinach

STALKS & SHOOTS

These vegetables provide juicy crunch and versatility. Served raw, for instance, celery and fennel offer a sweet crispness. By contrast, when cooked, they offer invaluable depth of flavour.

PREPARING ASPARAGUS

Always choose green asparagus with even-sized, smooth spears and tips that are tightly furled. The very thin variety known as sprue, which is prized for its piquant flavour, is prepared as shown here, but it does not need peeling as in step 2. For white asparagus, see box, right.

1 Snap off the pale woody ends of the asparagus. The spears should break easily where the pale flesh begins. Rinse the spears well in plenty of cold water, gently rubbing them free of any dirt.

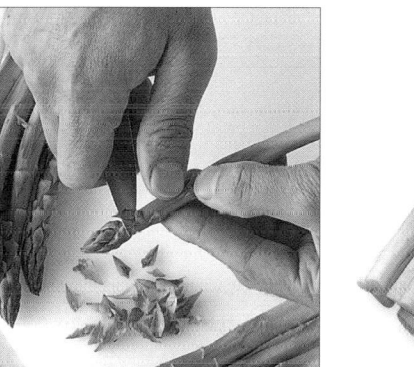

2 Carefully peel away the tough skin from the bottom half of the spears with a vegetable peeler.

3 Trim away the spiky leaves from the flower ends of the spears with the tip of a small knife.

4 Tie the spears into small bundles, making them easy to handle. To cook asparagus, see page 34.

To cook asparagus, see page 34.

OTHER STALKS AND SHOOTS

CARDOON: A Mediterranean favourite that looks like celery but is from the same family as globe artichoke, which it resembles in flavour. Discard outer stalks, strip away leaves and peel strings from ribs. The stalks will brown in contact with air, so keep cut stalks in acidulated water to combat this. Boiling is the best cooking method.

SWISS CHARD: A member of the beetroot family with thick white ribs and coarse leaves. Steam the stems, whole or sliced. Leaves are cooked separately, often as a substitute for spinach.

WHITE ASPARAGUS: A favourite Continental variety that grows underground and is fat with yellow tips. Must be peeled and cooked twice as long as green asparagus (see page 34).

(see page 34)

PREPARING CELERY

Only use crisp celery that snaps easily. Flexible sticks indicate staleness. Before using raw or cooked, any tough strings must be removed from the coarse outer sticks.

Trim the top and root ends from a bunch of celery, cutting off any green leaves and reserving them for garnishing. Separate into sticks. Peel the tough strings from the sticks with a vegetable peeler.

PREPARING FENNEL

Keep pieces of cut fennel in iced water – they brown when exposed to air. For flavour, choose mature bulbs that are well-rounded and plump.

Trim the top and root end of the fennel bulb, saving any green fronds for garnishing. Rinse the bulb. To cut into chunks, cut lengthwise in half. Cut each half into quarters. To slice, cut the bulb in half lengthwise and place cut-side down. Cut crosswise into slices.

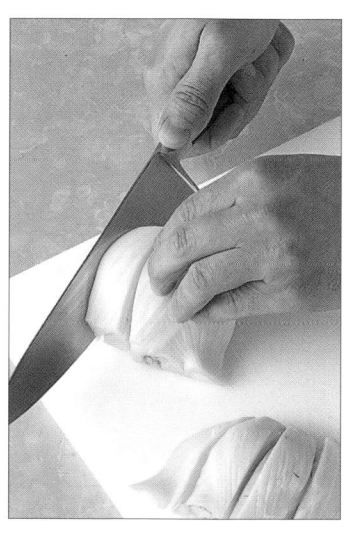

GLOBE ARTICHOKES

These are members of the thistle family. What we eat are actually the flower buds, which can be put to different uses depending on the way they are prepared. You can cook the whole artichoke or just the heart.

SERVING WHOLE ARTICHOKES

Boiled whole artichokes are traditionally used as a receptacle for dressings, into which the outer leaves are dipped. Some dressing ideas are listed here, plus more substantial fillings.

- Vinaigrette dressing.
- Flaked crab meat, mixed with mayonnaise and lemon juice.
- Lemon-butter sauce flavoured with finely snipped chives.
- Hollandaise sauce spiked with Dijon mustard and grated orange zest.
- *Tapenade* (olive purée) thinned with olive oil.
- *Aïoli*.
- Pesto stirred into finely chopped tomatoes, seasoned with red wine vinegar.
- Crème fraîche or fromage frais dressing flavoured with chopped fresh dill.

PREPARING AND COOKING WHOLE ARTICHOKES

In mature artichokes, sets of green fleshy leaves tightly enclose the tender heart and purple hairy choke. Only the base of these leaves, the heart and sometimes the stalk (see box, below) are edible. Mature artichokes are always served cooked.

1 Hold the artichoke firmly and break off the stalk at the bottom, pulling out the tough fibres that are attached to it.

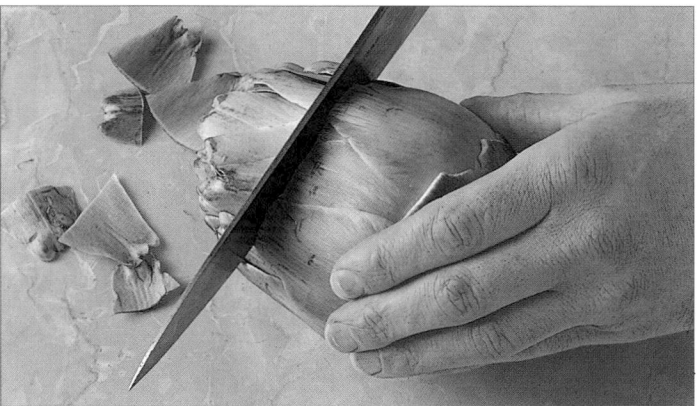

2 Cut off the top third of the artichoke and trim any tough outer leaves; discard. Place artichokes in a pan of boiling salted water with the juice of 1 lemon. Weight down with a plate and simmer for 20–35 minutes, depending on size.

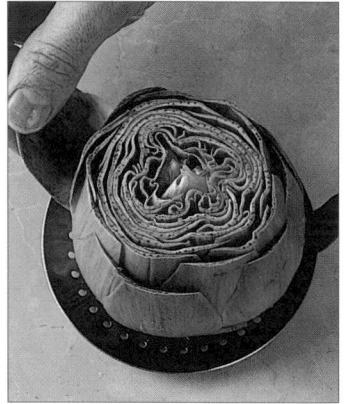

3 Test for doneness by pulling gently at one of the leaves, which should come away easily.

TRICK OF THE TRADE

WASTE NOT, WANT NOT

The stalks of very fresh, young artichokes are deliciously tender when cooked if they have been properly prepared.

For best results, simply peel off the outer fibrous layer with a small paring knife, then cut lengthwise into sticks. Cook in boiling salted water with a squeeze of lemon juice to help retain colour.

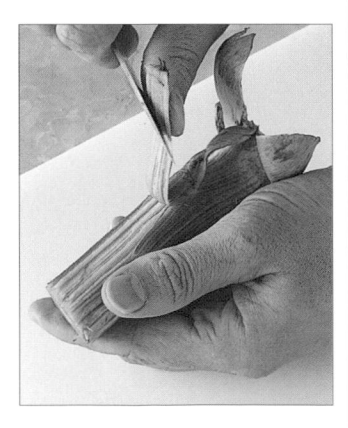

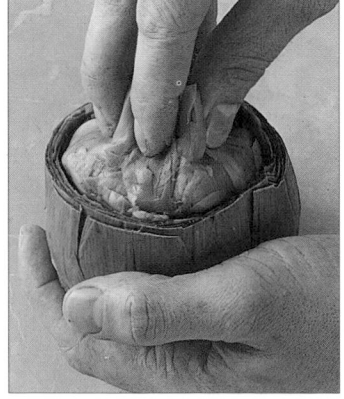

4 Pull out the central cone of leaves and reserve. Remove the hairy choke with a spoon and discard.

5 Put the cone back in the artichoke, upside-down. Spoon in a filling of your choice (see box, above left).

PREPARING ARTICHOKE HEARTS

The heart or bottom of the artichoke is the tenderest, most delicious part, often eaten on its own without the outer leaves. In classic French cuisine, hearts are simmered in a blanc (a stock containing flour and lemon juice) to help them keep their colour, but this is not absolutely essential. After cooking, serve hearts whole with a sauce or stuffing in the centre, or slice and toss in a dressing.

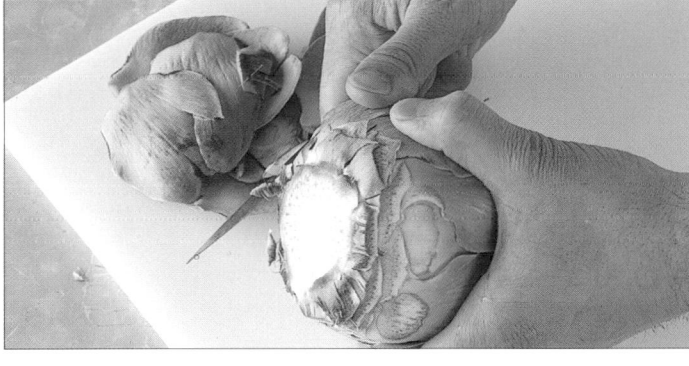

1 Carefully trim off the tough outer green leaves from the artichoke with a chef's knife. Break off the stalk with your hands, then cut the base flat.

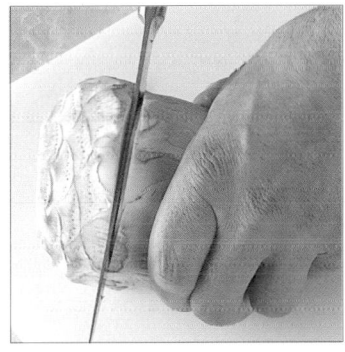

2 Hold the artichoke firmly and cut off the bottom third, taking care to include the heart; discard the top two-thirds.

3 Put the artichoke hearts in a bowl of cold water with half a lemon. This will help to prevent the artichokes from discolouring.

4 Place the hearts in a pan of boiling salted water, weight down with a plate and simmer for 15–20 minutes.

5 Test for doneness by piercing the heart with the tip of a paring knife. Drain well. When cool enough to handle, scoop out the hairy choke with a melon baller, and discard.

BABY ARTICHOKES

Baby artichokes are a particular delicacy. They can be eaten whole including the stalk and outer leaves and even the choke, which is barely developed. Here are some serving suggestions.

- Boil them for 3–4 minutes until tender, quarter them and serve warm with a vinaigrette dressing.
- Thinly slice them raw, then mix with olives and cherry tomatoes and dress with fruity extra-virgin olive oil and coarsely ground sea salt.
- Fry them whole in olive oil to make the Italian speciality *carciofi alla giudea*.
- Halve them and bake in a sauce made of fresh tomatoes, garlic, olive oil and basil.
- Simmer them until tender in water with olive oil, lemon juice, thyme, bay leaves and coriander seeds to make *artichauts à la grecque*. Let them cool in the liquid before draining and serving.

ROOTS & TUBERS

Beetroot, carrot, parsnip, turnip, radish and salsify all grow underground, hence their name and their hard fibrous constitution. Knobbly vegetables – celeriac, Jerusalem artichokes and kohlrabi – are included in the same category, and have similar techniques.

MAKING JULIENNE

Most root vegetables, such as the turnips illustrated here, have firm flesh suitable for cutting into long, thin sticks known as julienne. Prepared this way they need only brief cooking – boiling, steaming or sautéing – and make attractive garnishes.

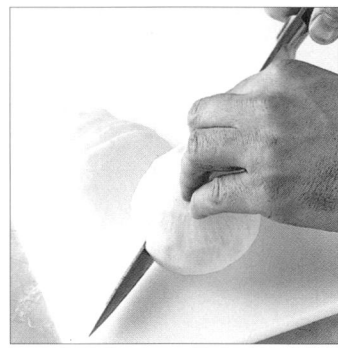 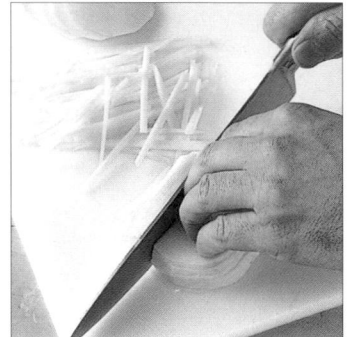

1 Peel the vegetable and cut it into thin slices with a chef's knife.

2 Stack the slices, a few at a time, and cut into thin, even-sized strips.

DICING

This produces even-sized cubes that cook quickly and make a neat and attractive presentation. Diced vegetables are often used as a base for soups and stews (see box, right), and are good for puréeing. Sweet potato is illustrated here.

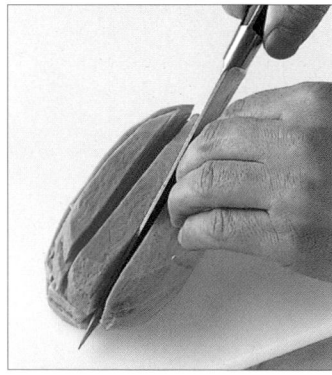 

1 Peel the vegetable and cut into even slices. Stack the slices, a few at a time, and cut lengthwise to make equal-sized bâtons.

2 Cut across the bâtons to make equal-sized dice. The size of the dice may vary (see box, right).

ROLL CUTTING

This method of cutting, favoured in Asian cooking, produces uniform pieces with maximum surface area. This is ideal for quick-cooking methods such as stir-frying and sautéing. Long roots, such as the carrot shown here, are best suited to this technique.

Peel the vegetable and top and tail. Starting at one end, cut at a 45° angle. Roll the carrot through 90° and cut at the same angle again. Repeat along the length of the carrot.

TRICK OF THE TRADE

MAKING MIREPOIX AND BRUNOISE

These diced vegetable preparations are classics in French cooking. Mirepoix, a basic flavouring for soups and stews, takes its name from its creator, the 18th-century Duc de Lévis-Mirepoix. Brunoise is the classic consommé garnish.

Mirepoix is a roughly diced mixture of raw carrot, onion and celery. Leek is also often included.

Brunoise is very finely diced raw carrot, celery, leek or courgette. Use singly or mix together.

MAKING RIBBONS

These are thin shavings made with a vegetable peeler. The technique is perfect for long root vegetables, especially carrots, because they have a hard, fibrous texture, and also for courgettes. Use vegetable ribbons as a side dish, and in salads and stir-fries. They also make an attractive garnish.

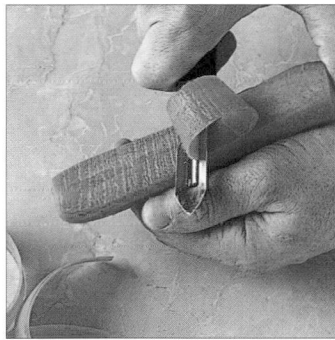

Peel the vegetable and discard the peelings. Holding the vegetable firmly in one hand, peel it all along its length with a vegetable peeler, using firm pressure. If the ribbons are not to be used immediately, keep them in iced water.

MANDOLIN

For slicing firm vegetables, such as roots and tubers, you can use a mandolin, called *mandoline* in French. The professional type is made of stainless steel (see below and page 17). It has one straight blade, coarse and fine shredding blades, and a rippled cutter for making *pommes gaufrettes* (see page 17). It also has a carriage to protect your fingers and steady the vegetable.

Simpler mandolins are made of wood with steel blades (see above). You can use the mandolin to slice very rapidly by placing the vegetable in the carriage and moving it back and forth over the blade. The thickness of the slices is adjustable.

TURNING

This classic French technique "turns" vegetables into neat barrel or olive shapes, traditionally with five or seven sides, to resemble baby vegetables. Turnips and carrots are turned here; potatoes, celeriac, courgettes and cucumber can also be prepared this way.

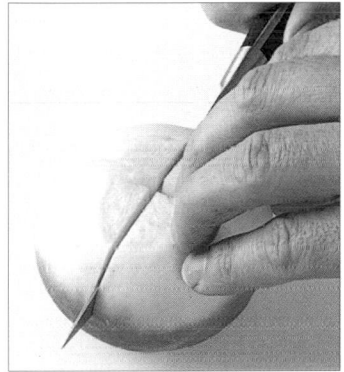

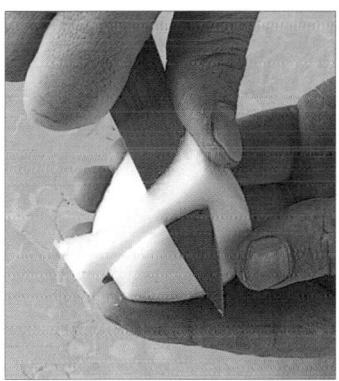

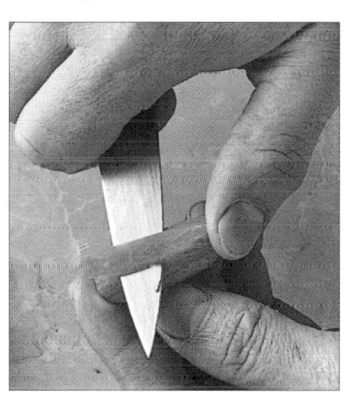

1 Cut round vegetables into quarters, tubular vegetables such as carrots into 5-cm lengths.

2 Carefully trim off all of the sharp edges, using a small paring knife, to form a curved shape.

3 Pare down the vegetable from top to bottom, turning it slightly after each cut until it is barrel-shaped.

PREPARING KNOBBLY VEGETABLES

Celeriac, Jerusalem artichokes and kohlrabi are all knobbly vegetables that look difficult to deal with, but the technique of preparing them is remarkably simple. First peel off the skin with a small paring knife, then slice, chop, shred or grate the flesh, depending on future use (see box, right). Once the flesh is cut, immerse the pieces in acidulated water immediately to prevent discoloration (see box, page 9).

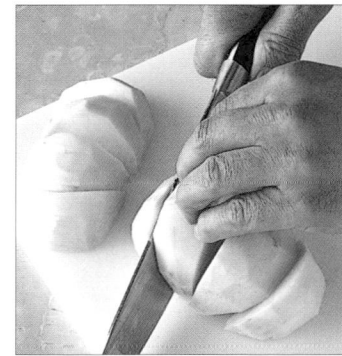

SLICING KOHLRABI
Cut the kohlrabi in half lengthwise, place each half cut-side down on a cutting board and cut into quarters.

SHREDDING CELERIAC
Set the coarse shredding blade of a mandolin (see box, above) to 5-mm thickness. Work the celeriac against the blade.

KNOBBLY VEGETABLES

Despite their strange appearance, knobbly vegetables are as versatile as potatoes.

- Slice or chop, then boil or steam. Toss in butter or olive oil and chopped fresh herbs.
- Slice or chop, then par-boil. Roast with herbs and seasoning.
- Slice or chop, then boil and mash with butter or olive oil, crushed garlic and seasoning.
- Shred or grate raw and toss in vinaigrette or mayonnaise.

POTATOES

Although potatoes appear in many shapes and colours (see box, opposite page), they fall into two basic categories – waxy and floury. For best results it is crucial to choose the right variety. Waxy potatoes have a high moisture and low starch content, ideal for sautéing, boiling and salads. Floury varieties have more starch, hence a light, fluffy texture. They are the prized "bakers" and offer the creamiest results in purées and gratins.

EXOTIC VEGETABLE

Potatoes are commonplace vegetables today but at one time they were as exotic as yams or eddoes are now. A staple food of the Peruvian Incas, they were brought to England in the 16th century by Sir Francis Drake. Surprisingly, at first they were thought fit only for animals, and were held responsible for diseases such as leprosy.

Sir Francis Drake (1540-1596)

SCRUBBING

Potato skins are full of nutrients and flavour, so it is best not to remove them before cooking. Scrub or scrape clean rather than peel.

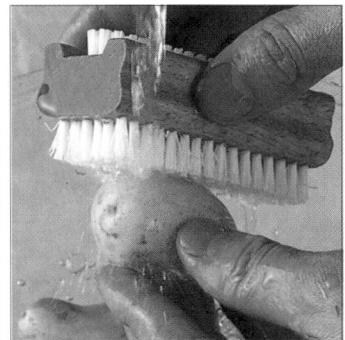

Hold the potato under cold running water and remove "eyes" with a knife tip. Scrub the skins all over with a stiff brush to remove any earth.

PREPARING FOR ROASTING

Potatoes can be roasted unpeeled or peeled. Small potatoes can be left whole, but for even and quick cooking, large potatoes are best prepared hasselback-style, or cut into smaller shapes. Pommes châteaux are the classic French shape. For two different roasting techniques, see pages 36 and 37.

HASSELBACK
Slice off the bottom of the potato to steady it. Make thin parallel cuts from the top almost to the bottom.

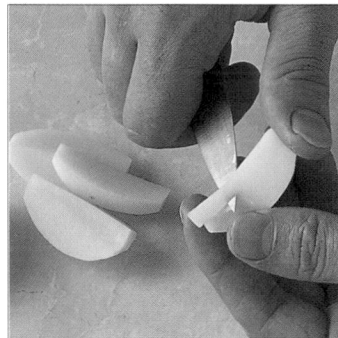

POMMES CHATEAUX
Cut potato lengthwise into quarters with a chef's knife. Shave off the flat edge of each quarter to round it.

PRICKING FOR BAKING

Large, floury potatoes are best for baking in the oven in their jackets. To prevent them bursting during cooking, the skin should be pierced by pricking it with a fork. If you like, rub with oil and salt to crisp the skin during cooking, or bake them on a bed of salt. You can also cook them on metal skewers – the heat is conducted through to the centre of the potatoes quicker this way.

Scrub potatoes (see above) and prick them all over with a fork, piercing right through to the flesh. Bake at 220°C, 1–1¼ hours.

MAKING POMMES PARISIENNES

This is the classic French way to prepare potatoes for sautéing. The name comes from the melon baller used to cut the potatoes, called cuillère parisienne or Parisian spoon. It produces small balls that cook in butter, or a mixture of butter and oil, to an even brown colour. Large floury potatoes are best – they produce a crisper result than waxy potatoes.

Press a melon baller into peeled potato and scoop out as many balls as possible. Drop the balls into a bowl of cold water as you work.

PREPARING POTATOES FOR DEEP-FRYING

There are many ways potatoes can be prepared for deep-frying, from ordinary chips to elaborate latticed potatoes or gaufrettes. They are usually peeled first, and must always be uniform in size and thickness. Drop them into cold water as you cut them to prevent discoloration. This also removes some of the starch and helps to make them crisp. Drain the shapes and dry them thoroughly before immersing in hot oil – see page 39 for the technique of deep-frying potatoes.

BY HAND

A sharp chef's knife can be used to cut thick sticks, such as the pommes pont neuf *shown here.* Pommes frites *and* allumettes *can also be cut by hand, but they are easier and more regular cut on a mandolin.*

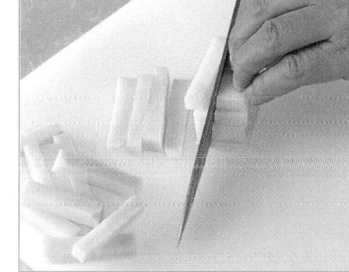

POMMES PONT NEUF
Named after the oldest bridge in Paris, these are always served stacked. Trim the ends and sides of potato to make a rectangular block, then slice 1 cm thick. Stack the slices and cut into sticks 1 cm wide.

BY MACHINE

A mandolin, with its choice of blades and cutters, is the best tool to use for these classic wafer-thin French fries. See the box on page 15 for information on mandolins.

POMMES ALLUMETTES
Work potato against the fine shredding blade set to 3-mm thickness. *Pommes pailles* (straw potatoes) are made in the same way, with the ramp positioned in line with the straight blade.

POMMES FRITES
Work potato against the coarse shredding blade set to 5-mm thickness.

POMMES GAUFRETTES
Work potato against the rippled cutter set to 1-mm thickness and discard the first slice. Turn the potato 90° and cut the next slice. Repeat along the potato, turning it 90° after each slice.

POMMES SOUFFLES
Slightly thicker than game chips. Work potato against the straight blade set to 3-mm thickness.

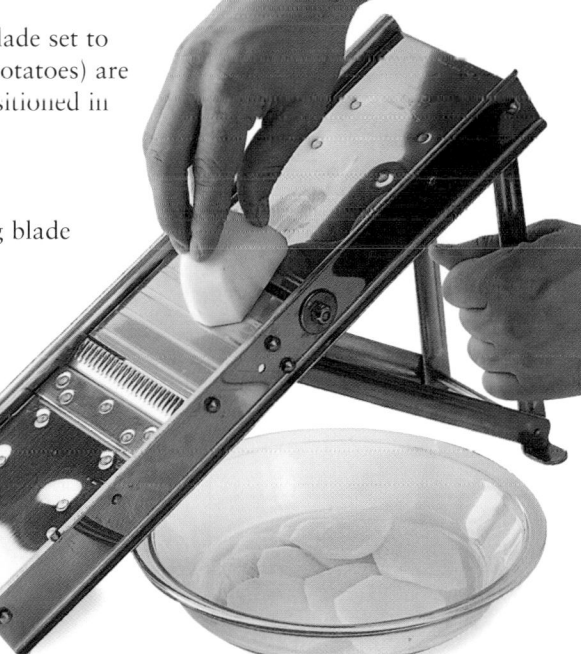

OLD POTATOES

These are available from September to June. Their starch content increases with maturity.

CARA: White skins and flesh, moist texture. For boiling, baking.
DESIREE: Red skins, pale flesh. For boiling, frying, baking.
KING EDWARD: White skins with pink patches, floury texture. For mashing, frying, roasting, baking.
MARIS PIPER: White skins, cream flesh, floury texture. For boiling, frying, roasting, baking.
PENTLAND SQUIRE: White skins, cream flesh, floury texture. For mashing, roasting, baking.
ROMANO RED: Red skins, cream flesh, soft dry texture. For boiling.

NEW POTATOES

These appear from early May and are still immature. They have a sweet flavour and waxy texture.

ESTIMA: Pale yellow skins, pale creamy flesh, firm moist texture. For boiling, frying, baking.
JERSEY: Yellow skin, creamy waxy flesh. For boiling, salads.
MARIS BARD: White skins, white to cream flesh. For boiling, salads.
ROCKET: White skin, white, firm waxy flesh. For boiling, salads.
WILJA: Yellow skins, pale yellow flesh, firm dryish texture. For boiling, mashing, frying, baking.

ALLUMETTES

FRITES

PONT NEUF

GAUFRETTES

SOUFFLES

MUSHROOMS

The term "mushroom" is used loosely to mean the whole family of edible fungi. There are three broad categories: common cultivated white mushrooms, exotic cultivated ones such as shiitake and oyster mushrooms, and wild fungi such as chanterelles, ceps and truffles.

TRICK OF THE TRADE

FINELY CHOPPING MUSHROOMS

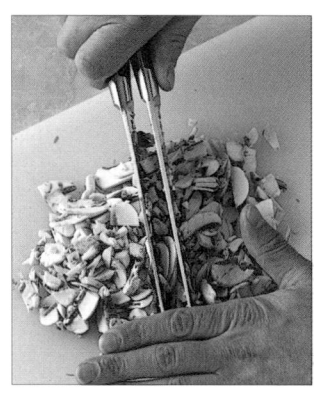

A quick method of chopping mushrooms for duxelles is to use two chef's knives held together in one hand. Secure the tips of the blades with your other hand and then chop, using a rocking motion. This limits the time the mushrooms are exposed to air and helps prevent discoloration. For a whiter duxelles, use only the mushroom caps.

PREPARING CULTIVATED MUSHROOMS

Mushrooms can be eaten raw or cooked. Ordinary white mushrooms are grown in pasteurized compost, so need only wiping. If very dirty, rinse briefly. Do not soak them or they will become soggy. Button mushrooms can be left whole or halved, larger ones may be sliced or chopped.

1 Trim off the woody ends of the stalks with a small knife. Save the trimmings for use in stocks and soups.

2 Wipe the mushrooms gently with damp paper towels, removing any compost still clinging to them.

SLICING
Put the mushrooms stalk-side down on a cutting board. Slice lengthwise with a chef's knife.

PREPARING WILD MUSHROOMS

Fresh wild mushrooms deteriorate quickly, so use them as soon as possible. If storing briefly, keep them in a paper bag in the refrigerator. Most wild mushrooms do not need washing or peeling, but check with your supplier.

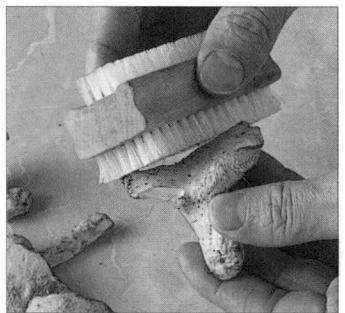

1 Gently brush off any earth that is still clinging to the mushrooms with a small brush or a clean cloth. Be careful not to damage the delicate flesh of the caps.

2 Trim off the woody ends of the stalks with a small knife. Leave as much of the flesh as possible. Many wild mushrooms are left whole or simply halved lengthwise, to preserve their attractive shape, but they can also be sliced in the same way as cultivated mushrooms.

PREPARING WOOD EARS

Also known as cloud ears, wood ears are an Asian fungus, commonly sold in dried form. Like dried mushrooms below, they must be reconstituted before use, when they swell into clusters of dark gelatinous lobes up to five times their dried size. They are used in stir-fries, soups and braised dishes.

Soak wood ears as for dried mushrooms below, then rinse thoroughly under cold running water to rid them of sand and grit lodged in the crevices. Dry thoroughly with a tea towel before use and trim off and discard the hard central stalks. Slice or chop wood ears according to individual recipe instructions.

WILD MUSHROOMS

CEP: *Porcini* "little pig" in Italian, this variety has a chubby shape and bulbous cap.
CHANTERELLE: Golden-hued and concave, tasting of apricots.
MOREL: A slim conical cap and honeycomb exterior, with a sweet intensity to rival truffles.
PIED DE MOUTON (OR HEDGEHOG): Cream-coloured and fleshy with tiny white spines under the gills.

RECONSTITUTING DRIED MUSHROOMS

Many different varieties of mushroom can be bought dried. These include Asian varieties such as shiitake and oyster mushrooms, and wild ones such as morels, ceps and chanterelles. Dried wild mushrooms are expensive but their flavour is highly concentrated, so even a very small quantity added to a dish will give a superb richness and depth. Add to dishes such as sauces, soups, omelettes, risottos, pasta sauces and stir-fries.

1 Put mushrooms in a bowl and cover with warm water. Leave to soak for 35–40 minutes or until they have softened.

2 Drain, then squeeze to extract the liquid. Strain the liquid and use with mushrooms.

SAFETY FIRST

If you pick wild mushrooms yourself, do not eat anything you cannot positively identify as being edible. Eat wild mushrooms as soon as possible as they quickly deteriorate.

TRUFFLES

There are two main types – the French black truffle from Périgord and the white truffle from Piedmont, northern Italy. The black truffle is eaten raw, used in stuffings and sauces, and braised or baked in pastry. White truffles are usually eaten raw.

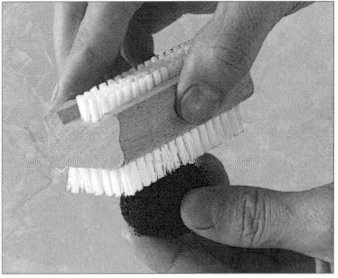

CLEANING A BLACK TRUFFLE
Carefully scrub the truffle with a brush. If you like, peel off the knobbly skin with a vegetable peeler, finely chop the peelings and use in cooked dishes.

SLICING A TRUFFLE
Shave black or white truffles as thinly as possible with a vegetable peeler. Use shavings in cooking, or sprinkled raw on dishes like pasta, risotto, polenta and omelettes.

From top to bottom, left to right: shiitake; pied bleu; chanterelle, wood ears; pied de mouton

PODS

This classification divides into two types: those that are eaten young and still in the pod, such as mangetouts, runner beans, French beans and okra; and those where the seeds are left to mature and are served shelled, such as garden peas and broad beans.

TESTING FOR FRESHNESS

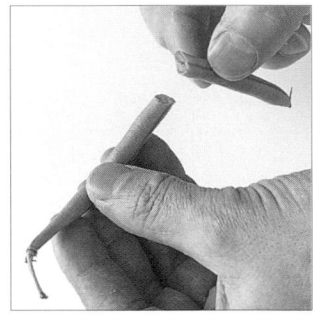

Most fresh green beans, with the exception of broad beans and very young French beans, should snap easily when bent in half. If they do not snap, they have been picked when too old or stored for too long.

PEAS

Some pea varieties, such as mangetouts and sugar snap, are cultivated to be harvested young and eaten in the pod. They need only to be stringed before being used raw in salads, or cooked. Other peas are picked later, when the pods are full. They are shelled and the pods discarded. Both types are best cooked briefly, either steamed, boiled or stir-fried.

STRINGING
For mangetouts and sugar snaps, break off the stalk and pull off the string.

SHELLING
Press the base of pea pods to open, then push your thumb up the pod, removing peas.

GREEN BEANS

Runner beans and French beans are eaten whole, including the pod. Runner beans are wide and flat, each containing several mottled purple seeds. They should be trimmed, stringed and sliced before cooking. French beans are long and cylindrical and simply need topping and tailing. They can be left whole, cut into short lengths or sliced on the diagonal.

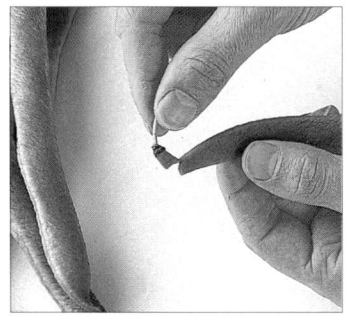

1 Snap the stalk off runner bean and pull the string down the pod. Repeat from the other end.

2 Slice beans diagonally with a chef's knife. Cut thinner slices for quick cooking, such as stir-frying.

BROAD BEANS

Young broad beans are soft and tender, and can be eaten whole. Always boil or steam them first, as certain beans contain toxins which are only neutralized in cooking. Mature pods are tough, and the beans need to be shelled and skinned following the method here.

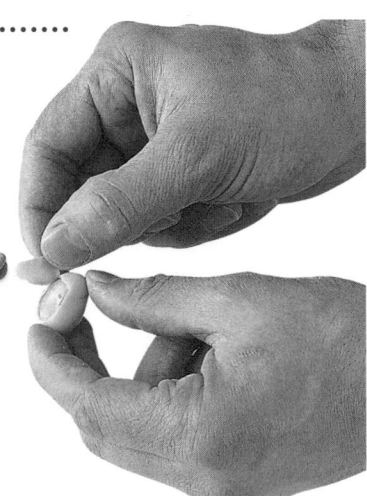

Shell mature beans as for peas (see above) and discard the pods. To remove the skins, first blanch beans, then slit the skin around one end using a small knife. Press the other end between your fingers and squeeze the bean out.

OKRA

Also known as "ladies' fingers" and bhindi, *okra are served cooked, usually whole in stir-fries, sliced in curries and stews. They are popular in Caribbean cooking for their natural thickening properties (see box, right).*

To cook whole okra, cut off the end of the stalk. Trim around the stalk to make a cone shape. This prevents the pod being pierced and releasing its sticky juices (see box, right).

SWEETCORN

Every part of sweetcorn may be used. Traditionally, the husked corn is boiled and served "on the cob" with butter, or the kernels are scraped off and cooked. In Mexican cooking, the husks are used to make *tamales*.

COBS AND KERNELS

Sweetcorn can be boiled or barbecued "on the cob", in which case only the husks and silks are removed, or the kernels can be stripped off and cooked separately.

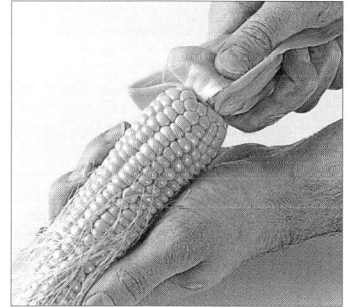

1 To husk the corn, grasp the leaves and pull them firmly back and off the cob.

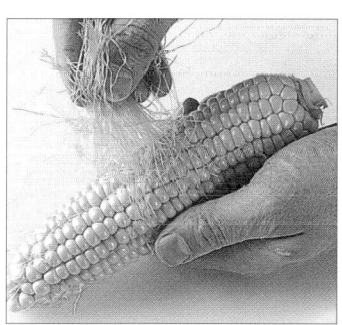

2 Pull off the silk. The corn is now ready for cooking whole "on the cob".

3 To strip the kernels, hold the cob stalk-end down. Cut down in smooth strokes.

USING CORN HUSKS

In Mexico, dried corn husks are used to make tamales *(see recipe box, right). Dried corn husks are not available here, so fresh corn husks are used instead. After removing them from the cobs (see step 1, above), dry them out in the oven at 150°C for about 30 minutes.*

1 Press a piece of cornmeal dough into the widest end of each corn husk with your fingers. Spoon a little of the spicy filling on top of it.

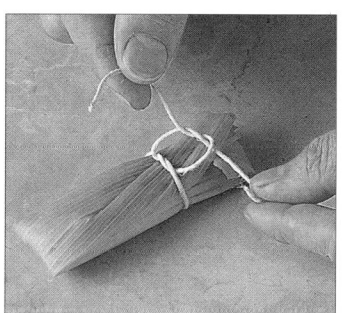

2 Wrap the long sides of the corn husk over the filling. Fold over the short ends and then tie the package neatly with kitchen string.

TAMALES

40 dried or fresh corn husks
175 g lard
450 g ground cornmeal
3 garlic cloves, chopped
1 onion, chopped
¼ tsp ground cloves
¼ tsp ground cinnamon
2 tbsp butter
450 g minced pork
1 red chilli, deseeded and
   finely chopped
Salt and freshly ground pepper

If using dried corn husks, soak them in cold water for 1 hour. Lay the husks flat to dry before filling. Mix the lard and cornmeal to form a dough. Press a small piece of dough into the widest end of each husk to make a rectangle.

For the filling, sweat the garlic, onion and spices in the butter. Add the pork and chilli. Cook until the pork browns, 5 minutes. Season well. Spoon the filling along the centre of the dough.

Wrap the husks around the filling and tie with string. Steam for 1 hour. Remove the string before serving. Peel open the husks – the filling is eaten with the fingers.

THE ONION FAMILY

Members of the onion family are essential to so many dishes, either as a subtle flavouring or as the star ingredient. When they are prepared correctly, following the methods shown here, they will release their flavour more readily and be more easily digested.

Once they are cut, the smell of onions can become quite overpowering, and volatile oils released can sting the eyes and make them water. A few time-honoured remedies may help to alleviate the problem.

One method is to peel onions while they are submerged in a bowl of water and then to keep the tap running while chopping.

Another technique is to leave the root end intact during chopping (see below). Chewing a piece of bread while slicing or dicing may also help.

PEELING AND SLICING ONIONS

All onions must be peeled before use to remove the papery skin. Here the technique of slicing a whole onion into rings is shown. For smaller, half-moon slices, cut the onion in half lengthwise, place cut-side down and cut into vertical slices.

1 Trim away the root end without cutting right through. Peel off the skin with a small knife.

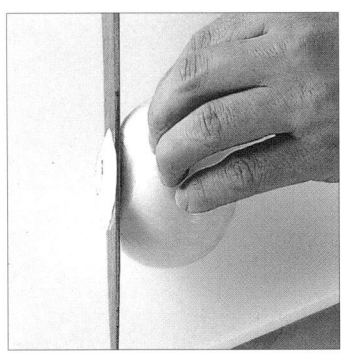

2 Cut off the tough root end with a chef's knife. Reserve for using in stocks.

3 Hold the onion on its side and slice downwards to form rings. Separate into individual rings, if you like.

DICING ONIONS

Many recipes call for onions to be diced or chopped. The size of the dice depends on the thickness of the first cuts. Keep the root end intact to prevent the onion from falling apart during chopping; it may also prevent tears (see box, above).

1 Cut peeled onion lengthwise in half. Place cut-side down and make a series of horizontal cuts without cutting the root.

2 Make a series of vertical cuts down through the onion, again making sure the root is not cut.

3 Hold the onion firmly on the cutting board and cut it crosswise into dice. For fine dice, continue to chop until the dice are the desired size. The tough root end that remains can be reserved for use in stocks.

PREPARING PEARL ONIONS

These small onions, also known as baby or button onions, are ideal for braising whole or pickling. The skins are thin and papery and can be difficult to remove. Steeping them in hot water first helps to loosen the skins before peeling.

1 Place the onions in a bowl and cover with hot water. Let steep for a few minutes until the skins begin to soften.

2 Drain the onions, rinse under cold running water, then peel away the skins with a small knife. Keep as much length to the stem ends as possible to prevent the centres from popping out. Discard skins.

CUTTING LEEKS

Trimmed leeks are often cooked whole or gently braised in stock or baked au gratin. Sliced leeks are baked in quiches or added to soups and stews. Diced leeks are used as a flavouring in classic French cooking (see mirepoix, page 14). If you are cooking leeks whole, they must be washed thoroughly to dislodge any earth that may be trapped between the tightly furled leaves.

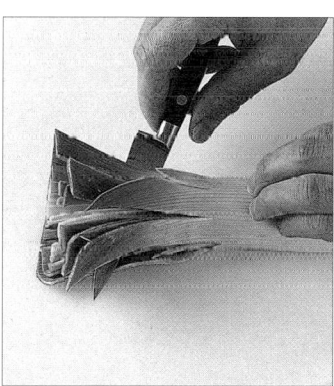

1 Slit the green tops. Rinse under cold running water to remove any trace of dirt.

2 Cut leek lengthwise in half. Lay leek flat and slice, thickly or thinly, across.

CRUSHING GARLIC

Choose firm, plump garlic heads and separate them into cloves before peeling.

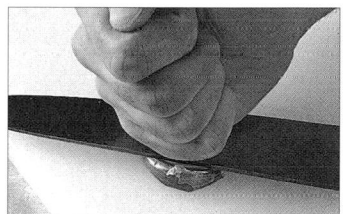

1 Lay the flat side of a chef's knife over a garlic clove and strike it with your fist.

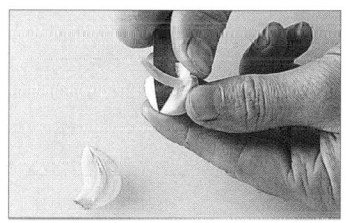

2 Peel the clove and cut it lengthwise in half. Remove the green shoot from centre.

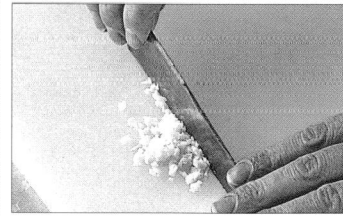

3 Finely chop the clove by moving the knife back and forth in a rocking motion.

CUTTING SPRING ONIONS ASIAN-STYLE

Spring onions are frequently used in Asian cooking, especially in quick stir-fries and soups. Sliced or shredded spring onions, using both the white and green parts, are also used as a flavouring ingredient and a garnish on hot dishes of rice or noodles, or sprinkled over steamed or braised fish and meat dishes.

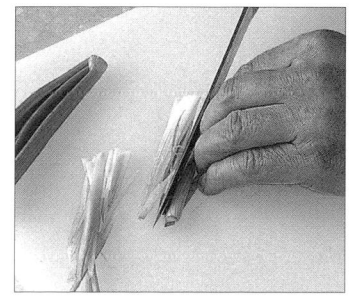

SHREDDING
Cut off the dark green top. Cut the light part lengthwise in half, then into strips.

ANGLE-SLICING
Start at the dark green top and slice at an angle, using the line of your knuckles as a guide. Slice right down to the root end; discard the root.

UNUSUAL VEGETABLES

Vegetables from Africa, Asia, South America and the Middle East are becoming more widely available. Sometimes these are exotic varieties of more familiar types like aubergines and radishes, but there are also completely new species which require different methods of preparation and cooking. Sea vegetables, in their dried form, are shown opposite.

1 AUBERGINES There are many varieties of aubergine apart from the familiar Mediterranean one. They are all prepared in the same way (see page 26).

2 WHITE & YELLOW AUBERGINES It would seems most likely that the alternative name for aubergine, eggplant, derives from this white variety from Africa, so named for its colouring and shape.

3 LOTUS ROOT Used in Chinese cooking, this vegetable cuts into attractive lacy slices. The skin must be peeled before cooking, then the flesh can be sliced and either steamed or stir-fried.

4 PEA AUBERGINES These are one of the more unusual types of aubergine from Thailand. Add whole to curries or purée for use in spicy dipping sauces.

5 DASHEEN The coarse skin of this tropical root must be peeled off before cooking. The flesh can then be cut into chunks and either baked or boiled.

6 CASSAVA This is a starchy potato-like root vegetable from Africa and South America. Peel and cook as for potatoes.

7 THAI AUBERGINE This green aubergine is prepared like white or purple aubergine (see above). The flesh should be sliced and then fried or roasted. It is also often used for pickling.

8 SALSIFY Also known as oyster plant because of its supposed similarity in taste to the seafood, the skin must be scraped off before the flesh is cooked. To cook, cut into short lengths and boil.

DRIED SEAWEEDS

1 WAKAME Mild in flavour. Good in salads, soups and stir-fries. Can also be toasted and crumbled, over rice dishes.

2 ARAME Delicately flavoured. Used in Japanese *miso* soup.

3 KOMBU A dried form of kelp used in the making of Japanese *dashi* (seaweed stock).

4 DULSE Salty and spicy tasting, this is particularly good in stir-fries and in salads.

9 MOOLI This vegetable, also called white radish and daikon, is much used in Asian cooking. It can be either shredded and eaten raw or thinly sliced and stir-fried or steamed.

10 LOOFAH An edible gourd generally used in Asian cooking, this vegetable must be peeled before cooking and can then be steamed or stir-fried.

11 CHINESE BITTER MELON A Far Eastern edible gourd, the flesh must be salted (dégorgéd) in order to draw out the bitter juices. The flesh is then best either sautéd or stir-fried.

12 EAST INDIAN ARROWROOT A hard root with tough skin, this is used in South-east Asian stir-fried dishes. Once peeled the flesh can be shredded or diced.

13 EDDO This is a tuber from West Africa and the Caribbean, which can be prepared and cooked like potatoes.

14 ICICLE RADISH Also called green radish, this rather bitter Asian vegetable is used for pickling and preserving but can also be thinly sliced for stir-frying.

15 YARD-LONG BEANS These are an Asian vegetable which can be cooked whole or sliced on the diagonal like runner beans.

16 TARO A hard mealy root vegetable from South-east Asia and India. Peel before cooking and cut into chunks or slices and boil.

17 KOHLRABI This is a slightly unusual European vegetable that should be prepared and cooked like turnip (see page 14).

VEGETABLE FRUITS

Considered fruits by botanists because they contain their own seeds, this colourful group is treated like vegetables in the kitchen. For peppers and chillies, which also contain their own seeds, see pages 28–29.

PEELING, DESEEDING AND CHOPPING TOMATOES

Although often eaten raw or baked in their skins, recipes for sauces, soups and stews often call for tomatoes to be peeled, deseeded and chopped – as in the French concassée of tomatoes. Core and score a cross in the bottoms before blanching. The bitter seeds are best removed.

1 Score cored tomatoes and blanch in boiling water for 10 seconds. Drain, then immerse in iced water.

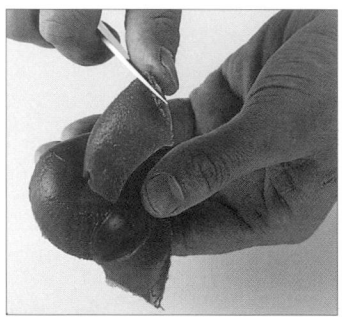

2 Remove tomatoes from the water and peel off the loosened skins, using the tip of a small knife.

3 Cut tomato in half. Taking each half in turn, squeeze out the seeds over a bowl. Remove any core.

4 Put each tomato half cut-side down and cut into strips, then cut across the strips to dice the flesh.

LOVE APPLES

Tomatoes arrived in Europe from the New World in the 1500s following Cortes' conquest of Mexico. One of their early names was "love apples", *pommes d'amour* in French. This may have derived from their reputation as an aphrodisiac. It is possible that early varieties were orange-yellow in colour, hence the corruption of the Italian *pomodoro* – "golden apple" or that the name *pomi di Mori* – "Moorish apples", reflected their route into Europe via Spain.

Cortes (1485-1547)

SALTING AUBERGINES

For most dishes, aubergines do not need peeling. However, they can contain bitter juices which are best extracted before cooking. This technique is called salting or dégorgéing, and is advisable if aubergines are to be fried in oil – it firms the flesh so that less oil is absorbed during cooking.

Slice the aubergine. Spread the slices in a single layer in a colander. Sprinkle salt evenly over the cut surfaces. Leave for about 30 minutes. Rinse under cold running water, then pat dry before cooking.

PREPARING AUBERGINES FOR BAKING

To ensure the flesh of of halved aubergines cooks evenly, the cut surfaces are deeply scored. You can perfume the flesh by inserting razor-thin slices of garlic into the incisions before baking.

Remove the stalk and calyx (the cup around the base of the stalk) and cut the aubergine in half lengthwise using a chef's knife. Cross-hatch the flesh deeply using a sharp pointed knife, then sprinkle with salt (see above).

PREPARING SQUASH

Soft-skinned summer squash that can be eaten raw like courgettes, and marrows, are often left unpeeled. Winter squash, such as pumpkin and butternut, have hard, thick skins which must be peeled, and a firm flesh that must be cooked. Small varieties can be halved before cooking; large squash are often cubed.

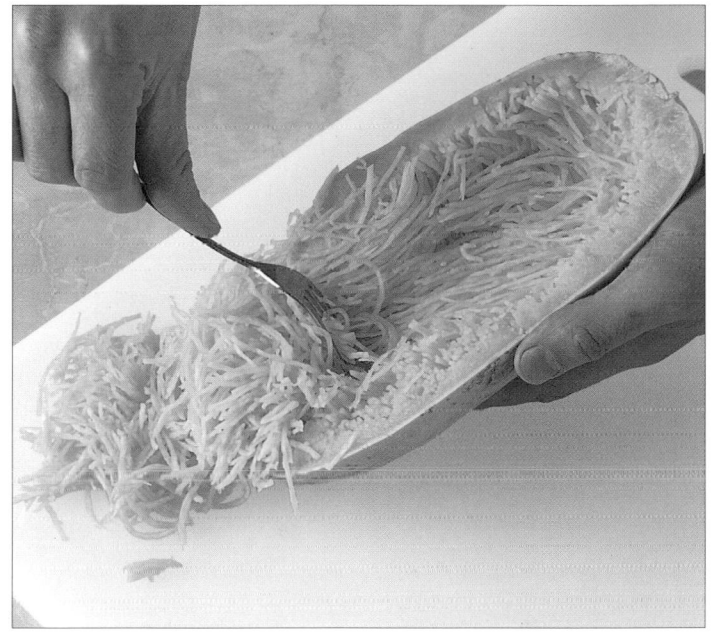

ACORN SQUASH
Cut squash in half lengthwise through the stalk. Scoop out seeds and fibrous pulp with a spoon, then peel off skin.

BUTTERNUT SQUASH
Cut squash in half. Peel or carve off the skin from each half, then cut the flesh into chunks.

SPAGHETTI SQUASH
Cut squash in half lengthwise and scoop out the seeds. Brush the cut surfaces with olive oil and season well. Bake at 180°C for 30 minutes. Rake out the flesh using a fork. It will form spaghetti-like strands.

PREPARING CUCUMBER

Mostly eaten raw, cucumbers can also be puréed in soups, stuffed and baked, or stir-fried. In classic French cooking the skin is always removed, and the flesh salted (dégorged).

For a decorative effect, pare evenly spaced narrow strips of skin lengthwise with a canelle knife. Slice cucumber crosswise, dégorge and drain before serving.

STONING AN AVOCADO

For avocados to be served as halves, with a dressing or filling in the central cavity, the skin is left intact. A chef's technique is shown here; a teaspoon can also be used.

Cut avocado lengthwise in half all around the stone. Twist halves in opposite directions until separated. Carefully strike stone with a chef's knife. Twist to dislodge.

PEELING AND SLICING AN AVOCADO

Avocados are usually served raw, but can also be lightly cooked. For purées and dips, the flesh is extracted from a halved and stoned pear (see left) and mashed. For salads, the flesh is peeled and sliced or diced. Using a stainless steel knife or spoon when cutting the flesh and brushing the cut surface with lemon juice helps prevent discoloration.

1 Score the skin of a whole avocado lengthwise into quarters, then lift the skin at one end and pull it back in strips, leaving behind as much flesh as possible.

2 Thinly slice the avocado down to and around the stone, lengthwise or crosswise, to remove the flesh. Brush the slices with lemon juice immediately.

PEPPERS

Sweet peppers or capsicums are related to chillies, but they have a mild, not hot, flavour that sweetens as they ripen. They are eaten raw and cooked, and are especially delicious when roasted (see page 37).

SLICING AND DICING PEPPERS

Peppers are kept whole only for stuffing and baking (see below), otherwise they are normally sliced into rings or cut into strips or dice for eating raw or cooked. They need to be cored, halved and deseeded before slicing and dicing.

1 Cut around the core with a small knife, pull out and discard. Cut the pepper lengthwise in half. Scrape out the seeds and ribs and discard.

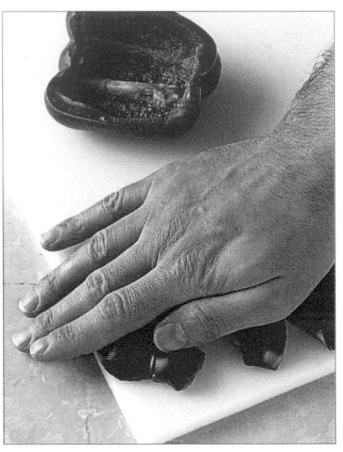

2 Place the pepper flesh-side down on a cutting board and press down firmly to flatten (this will make the pepper easy to slice).

3 Cut each pepper half lengthwise with a chef's knife into thin, even-sized slices or strips.

4 For diced pepper, hold the strips firmly together and slice crosswise to make equal-sized cubes. For larger dice, cut wider strips.

DIFFERENT COLOURS

Peppers come in a dizzying array of colours. Red and green are the most common, but yellow, orange, purple and even white are also available. Often varying hues simply denote peppers at different stages of ripeness. The familiar squat box-shaped pepper, for example, is least ripe when it is green. At this stage it has a fresh grassy flavour. As it matures its colour may change to either red, yellow, orange or purple, and its flavour become sweeter. In general, small green peppers are less sweet and juicy than large ones of other colours.

PREPARING WHOLE PEPPERS FOR BAKING

Sweet peppers make perfect containers for stuffing and baking. They are naturally hollow once the core and seeds have been removed, the sliced-off top makes a convenient lid, and the unskinned flesh will hold firm around the filling during baking. The technique shown here is also used for peppers that are to be sliced into rings.

1 Cut off the top quarter of the pepper that holds the stalk. Do not discard it but reserve it to use as a lid for the stuffed pepper during baking.

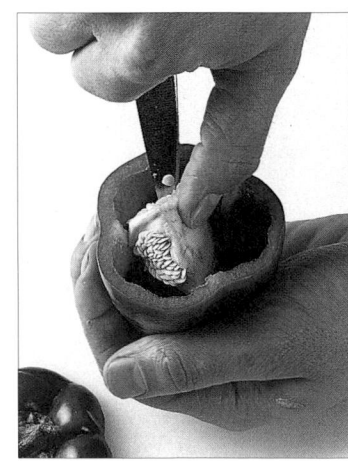

2 Scrape out the seeds with the tip of a small knife blade or a spoon. The pepper can now be filled and the lid replaced ready for baking.

CHILLIES

The often searingly hot properties of chillies call for careful handling. No matter what the variety, size or colour of the chilli, the preparation techniques are essentially the same.

PREPARING FRESH CHILLIES

Once cut open, chillies sting the skin (see box, right), so prepare them with care. Wash hands, knife and cutting board thoroughly afterwards, and take particular care not to touch your eyes. Some cooks wear rubber gloves for extra protection.

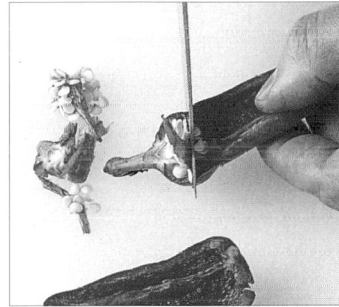

1 Cut chilli lengthwise in half. Scrape out the seeds with a small knife, removing the membrane with them.

2 Flatten the chilli with the palm of your hand and slice lengthwise into strips with a chef's knife.

3 For dice, hold the strips firmly together and slice into equal-sized cubes.

WHERE IS THE STING?

The intense fiery heat of chillies comes from the compound capsaicin. This oily substance is present to varying degrees in all parts of the chilli, but is strongest in the membrane and seeds inside the pod. For this reason, these parts are generally removed before cooking.

In some varieties of chilli, capsaicin neutralizes as the fruit ripens, making the heat less intense. As a general guide, green chillies are hotter than red and small chillies are hotter than large ones, but not always. Among the hottest are habañero and the tiny bird's-eye chillies. The mildest include sweet banana and the tapering green Anaheim chillies. Experiment with different kinds until you find those that best suit your needs — new varieties are constantly being introduced.

REHYDRATING DRIED CHILLIES

Use dried chillies as a substitute for fresh chillies in cooking. They can be crushed or simply crumbled (with or without the seeds), or soaked and ground into a paste as here.

1 Spread dried chillies out on a baking sheet and toast them under a hot grill for 3–5 minutes, turning them frequently.

2 Transfer chillies to a bowl and cover with warm water. Let stand for 1 hour.

3 Drain the chillies and grind them to a paste in a pestle and mortar, then rub the paste through a sieve to remove the skins.

From left to right, top: Scotch bonnet; Jalapeño; Serrano. **Bottom:** Habañero; Bird's-eye chilli; Caribe chilli

Chiles Rellenos

A popular classic from Mexico, chiles rellenos is literally translated as "stuffed peppers". Traditionally for festive occasions, the chillies are dipped in batter and deep-fried, and served as finger food at casual buffets. Here a lighter grilled version, without batter, is also given, so you can mix and match according to personal preference.

SERVES 6–8

26 assorted chillies (jalapeños, poblanos, red and yellow Anaheims, Scotch bonnets)

Vegetable oil, for frying

225 g Monterey Jack or Cheddar cheese, grated

225 g white crabmeat (fresh, defrosted or canned)

2 tbsp chopped fresh coriander

Juice of ¹/₂ lime

Prepare the chillies (see box, below). Heat 3 tbsp oil in a frying pan and fry the chillies for 3–5 minutes, turning them so they cook evenly on all sides. Work in batches to prevent the chillies from overcrowding the pan. Let drain on paper towels.

For cheese-stuffed chillies, press grated cheese into jalapeños and poblanos with your fingers, allowing about 1 tbsp cheese for jalapeños and 3 tbsp for poblanos.

For crab-stuffed chillies, pick over the crabmeat to remove any bits of shell or cartilage (if using frozen or canned crabmeat, drain it thoroughly first). Flake the crabmeat with a fork and mix in the chopped coriander and lime juice. Spoon the mixture into yellow Anaheim and Scotch bonnet chillies.

To grill (for all chillies): place chillies on a baking sheet and put under a hot grill for about 2 minutes, just until the cheese is melted.

To deep-fry (for stuffed jalapeños and poblanos and whole red Anaheims): make batter (see box, right). Heat about 8 mm oil in a large frying pan until it is very hot. Holding chillies by their stalks, dip them into the batter to coat, then deep-fry in batches in the hot oil until golden, 2–3 minutes for each batch. Drain on paper towels before serving.

BATTER FOR DEEP-FRIED CHILLIES

100 g plain flour
Pinch of salt
1 egg
100 ml milk

Sift the flour and salt into a bowl and make a well in the centre. Lightly beat the egg and pour into the well. Gradually begin to draw the flour from the sides into the egg, beating with a wooden spoon. When almost all incorporated, beat in the milk to make a smooth batter. If necessary, sieve the batter to remove any lumps.

Preparing Chillies

The technique shown here is suitable for jalapeños and poblanos, and red Anaheims if you like. It retains the shape of the chillies so they can be stuffed whole. For round-topped chillies such as yellow Anaheims and Scotch bonnets, cut off the tops and scoop out the cores and seeds. Keep the tops for presentation.

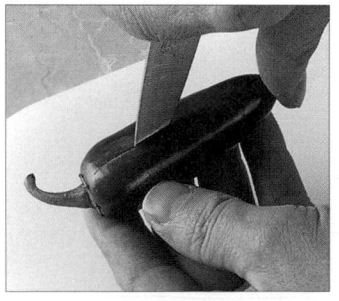

Make a lengthwise slit in the side of each chilli, from the shoulder down, using a small paring knife. With your fingers, carefully open out the slit to expose the seeds in the centre of the chilli.

Run your finger down the inside of the chilli to remove the seeds, starting from the shoulder. take care to wash your hands thoroughly afterwards or the juice from the chillies may sting.

SALAD LEAVES

A beautiful salad depends on more than just the mix of greens. The leaves must be fresh and crisp, and perfectly clean and dry. The techniques for achieving this are shown here.

PREPARING LETTUCE

Lettuces have a hard, bitter core which is best removed. The leaves should also be washed to remove dirt and then thoroughly dried. Water left on the leaves will cause them to wilt and dilute any dressing.

1 Discard any damaged outer leaves. Hold the head of the lettuce in one hand. Grasp the hard core in the other and twist it off.

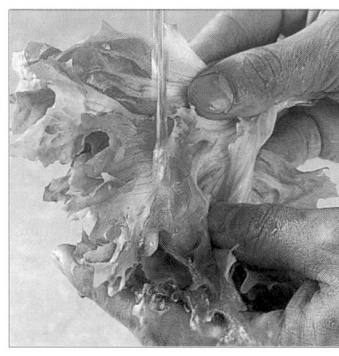

2 Rinse the leaves well under cold running water, then submerge them briefly in a bowl of cold water.

3 Place leaves in a folded tea towel and pat dry (or use a salad spinner, see box left). To crisp, refrigerate for at least 30 minutes.

Outer circle, clockwise from bottom left: red oak leaf; Iceberg; Cos lettuce; lollo rosso; curly leaf; radicchio; frisée; Little Gem lettuce. **Inner circle, clockwise from left:** lamb's lettuce; watercress; green lollo biondo. **Centre:** cress

MAKING A TOSSED SALAD

Choose leaves with flavours, colours and textures that are complementary. Whisk dressing in the salad bowl.

Tear leaves over the bowl; do not cut them or they will bruise. Toss leaves in dressing until lightly and evenly coated.

FRESH HERBS

Fresh herbs are aromatic plants that flavour and garnish both raw and cooked dishes. Here the techniques of chopping, shredding and snipping are shown. For other techniques using herbs, see pages 42–44.

PREPARING FRESH HERBS

For maximum flavour, use fresh herbs immediately after picking. Usually only the leaves are used, although stalks are also sometimes included. The aromas come from the essential oils, which are released by cutting.

CHOPPING
Strip the leaves from the stalks and chop coarsely, bunching the leaves up against a chef's knife.

SHREDDING
Suitable for soft leaves such as basil. Stack the leaves and roll them tightly. Slice crosswise into shreds.

SNIPPING CHIVES
Hold a bunch of chives over a bowl or board and finely snip them into small pieces with kitchen scissors.

FINES HERBES

This classic mixture of four herbs consists of equal quantities of chives, chervil, parsley and tarragon. The chives should be snipped and the other herbs finely chopped. Fine herbs should always be added at the end of cooking.

Snip chives (see above, right). Put chervil, parsley and tarragon leaves on a cutting board and chop them finely together. Combine with the chives before using.

MAKING A BOUQUET GARNI

The classic mix for this flavour enhancer is thyme, bay, parsley and celery wrapped in the dark green part of a leek and tied tightly with string. Used in slow-cooked dishes, it gradually releases its flavours.

For the bouquet garni shown here, the green part of the leek is loosely wrapped around a bay leaf, a sprig each of rosemary and thyme and a few stalks of parsley, then tied with string. For easy removal of a bouquet garni at the end of cooking, leave a long end on the string and tie it to the handle of the pan, or enclose the bouquet in a muslin bag.

BOILING

Boiling brings out the natural flavour of vegetables. Root vegetables should be added to cold water and slowly brought to the boil. By contrast, green vegetables should be plunged into rapidly boiling water.

ROOT VEGETABLES

It is important to cook root vegetables evenly through to the centre. Undercooked, they will be hard, overcooked they may lose texture and flavour, and even become mushy. For best results, cut them into equal-sized pieces and simmer slowly.

2 Simmer until tender, 12–20 minutes, depending on type. To test for doneness, pierce the centre of the root with the tip of a knife; it should meet no resistance.

1 Place vegetables in pan. Cover with cold water and add salt to taste. Bring slowly to the boil, then cover.

GREEN VEGETABLES

When boiled until just tender, green vegetables have a crisp bite, vibrant colour, optimum nutrients and the freshest flavour. If overcooked, they will turn drab and flabby.

1 Bring a large pan of water to the boil. Add salt to taste, then the vegetables. Simmer uncovered until just tender, 1–4 minutes.

2 Drain the vegetables and immerse in a bowl of iced water to refresh them. Drain and serve cold, or gently reheat with oil or butter.

ASPARAGUS

Asparagus is boiled upright so the thick ends of the stalks cook in simmering water while the tender tips gently steam above. The steamer here is designed specifically for the job, but you can cook asparagus flat, in a deep sauté pan.

Stand asparagus bundles (see page 11) upright in steamer basket. Pour water 10 cm deep into the steamer, bring to the boil and add salt to taste. Place basket in steamer, cover and simmer until stalks are tender, 5–7 minutes. Lift the basket out of the steamer, drain the asparagus and serve with melted butter or hollandaise sauce.

STEAMING

Steaming vegetables in the vapour produced by simmering water cooks them gently to crisp-tender perfection while retaining nutrients. You can use a sieve set over a pan, or one of the special steamers shown here.

CONVENTIONAL METHOD

A stainless steel pan with an inset basket for easy lifting makes light work of steaming a variety of vegetables together (carrots, pattypan squash and green beans are shown here). The water should simmer at a quivering, not rolling, boil. Do not sprinkle salt over the vegetables – it draws out moisture and may discolour them.

1 Bring 2.5 cm water to the boil in the bottom pan. Insert the basket containing the vegetables.

2 When the steam rises, cover the pan and cook the vegetables until tender (see chart, right).

3 Remove the basket and refresh the vegetables under cold running water. Reheat and season.

BAMBOO STEAMER METHOD

Asian-style bamboo steamers fit neatly over woks or other pans and can be stacked in tiers to steam different items separately. For delicately scented and flavoured vegetables, add seasonings such as a bouquet garni, mixed peppercorns, star anise, lemon grass and coriander to the water before steaming.

1 Place firm vegetables in bottom basket, tender ones in the top. Pour water into a wok to just cover the bottom; bring to the boil.

2 Place the stack of baskets on a trivet in the wok. Cover and steam until vegetables are tender (see box, above right).

ROASTING & BAKING

Many vegetables, particularly fibrous roots and tubers and vegetable fruits, are suited to roasting on their own or baking with an accompanying sauce. The long cooking time renders them tender and intensifies their flavour.

ROASTING TIMES

The times given below are for roasting vegetables in olive oil at 200°C (see opposite page). All times are approximate.

- AUBERGINES 30 mins

- CARROTS 45 mins

- PARSNIPS 30–45 mins

- SWEET POTATOES 45 mins

- TURNIPS 30–45 mins

- WINTER SQUASH 30–45 mins

ROASTING POTATOES

For a crisp and crunchy outside and soft creamy centre, the trick is to parboil the potatoes first, let them cool, and then roast them. Very hot oil and a very hot oven are essential. For an alternative, Continental, method of roasting potatoes, see opposite page.

 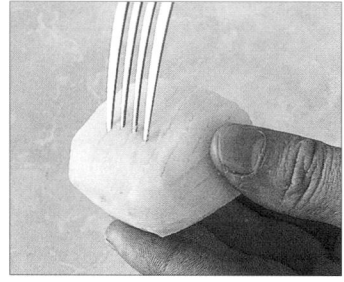 

1 Peel the potatoes. Leave small ones whole; cut large potatoes into chunks. Parboil in salted water for 10 minutes, then drain and let cool.

2 Scratch the potatoes with a fork (this helps make them crisp). Pour 1 cm oil into a roasting tin and heat at 200°C until very hot.

3 Add the potatoes and turn them to coat in the oil. Return the tin to the oven and roast the potatoes for 1–1¼ hours, turning them twice. Drain on paper towels.

ROAST GARLIC FLOWERS

Roasting mellows and sweetens the flavour of garlic so that it can be used as a delicious accompaniment as well as a flavouring. Roast whole heads of garlic in their skins at the same time as a joint of meat. If they are trimmed decoratively to form a flower, they also make very attractive garnishes.

Slice off the top of each head of garlic, cutting through the cloves. Place them cut-side up in a baking dish. Brush with olive oil and roast at 180°C for about 50 minutes.

ROASTING BEETROOT

Raw beetroot is left unpeeled for roasting so that the colour does not bleed. Cut off the tops, leaving the stalks intact.

Wrap beetroot in foil and roast at 150°C for 1–1½ hours. Let cool slightly and peel. Dot with butter and season with black pepper and coarsely ground sea salt before serving.

ROASTING PEPPERS

When peppers are roasted they acquire an intensely sweet, smoky flavour. The skin is always removed. The flesh, which becomes quite soft, is usually sliced or diced for eating as it is, or for use in composite dishes.

1 Put pepper in a roasting tin. Roast at 200°C, turning once, until skin is charred, 10–12 minutes.

2 Enclose the pepper in a plastic bag. Knot or seal the bag and leave until the pepper is cold.

3 Remove the pepper and core it. Lift the charred skin with a pointed knife, and peel it off.

TRICK OF THE TRADE

QUICK ROASTING
This time-saving method is ideal if you only need to roast one or two peppers.

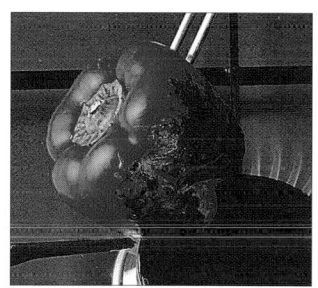

Spear the pepper with a long-handled fork. Hold it over a gas flame and turn it slowly, until the skin is blackened.

ROASTING IN OLIVE OIL

This quick-and-easy technique of roasting vegetables is most often used in Italy and France. For the best flavour, use a good-quality extra virgin olive oil, coarse sea salt, freshly ground black pepper and herbs such as rosemary or thyme.

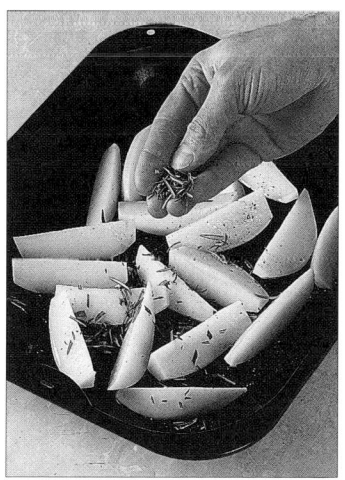

POTATOES
Put potato chunks (*pommes châteaux* are shown here, see page 16) in a roasting tin. Sprinkle with 2–4 tbsp olive oil, chopped fresh herbs and season with salt and pepper to taste; mix well. Roast at 200°C turning once or twice, until well browned, about 45 minutes.

RATATOUILLE
Put sliced courgettes, peppers, aubergines and onions in a roasting tin and add a bouquet garni (see page 33). Sprinkle with 3–4 tbsp olive oil, crushed garlic and salt and pepper to taste; mix well. Roast at 180°C for about 1 hour, turning once or twice.

MAKING A POTATO GRATIN

The term au gratin *refers to any dish topped with cheese and baked in a shallow dish until brown and crispy. The potatoes in the classic* gratin dauphinois *(see box, right), are parboiled in milk before baking. This lends a rich taste and ensures the potatoes cook in the required time.*

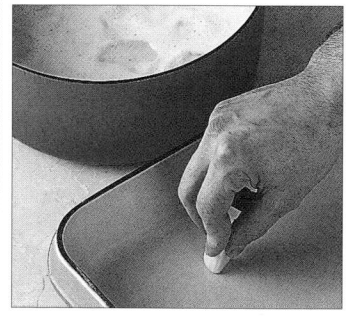

A HINT OF GARLIC
For a subtle garlic flavour, cut a garlic clove in half and rub the cut surfaces over the inside of baking dish. Garlic juices will not be as strong as the actual flesh.

GRATIN DAUPHINOIS

1 kg potatoes
1 bouquet garni
Freshly grated nutmeg
Salt and white pepper
500 ml milk
1 garlic clove, halved
25 g butter, softened
150 ml double cream
100 g Gruyère cheese, grated

Peel the potatoes and thinly slice them. Bring the milk to the boil in a pan. Add the bouquet garni, and nutmeg and salt and pepper to taste. Add the potatoes and return to the boil. Lower the heat and simmer for 10–15 minutes. Drain the potatoes and reserve the milk. Rub the garlic over the inside of a 22- × 33-cm baking dish. Butter the dish and layer the potatoes in it, seasoning each layer. Add the cream to the milk and to the boil and pour over the potatoes. Top with the grated Gruyère cheese and bake at 200°C for about 40 minutes. Serves 4.

FRYING

Vegetables can be shallow-fried, deep-fried or stir-fried; they are also fried as part of other cooking processes – in casserole making for example. All vegetables for frying must be cut into small pieces so they will not burn on the outside before the inside is cooked.

SWEATING AND GLAZING

These two techniques are often used in French cooking. Diced flavouring vegetables (see mirepoix, page 14) are sweated gently at the start of a soup or stew so they cook in their own juices and retain flavour without browning. Greaseproof paper is used as a covering to prevent evaporation – for a snug fit, it can be cut into a cartouche (see box, left). Glazing is the classic technique for finishing off turned vegetables (see page 15). It gives them an attractive glossy presentation.

SWEATING
Melt 1-2 tbsp butter in a pan. Add vegetables, sprinkle with water and seasonings. Cover with greasepoof paper. Cook over a low heat, 3-5 minutes.

GLAZING
Melt 2 tbsp butter with 1 tbsp water and 1 tsp sugar. Add blanched vegetables and cook over a high heat, rolling them until glazed, 2-3 minutes.

MAKING VEGETABLE FRITTERS

Vegetables cut into julienne and held together with batter can be shallow-fried to make crisp fritters or rösti. Here, a mixture of potatoes, carrots and courgettes are shown.

1 Make a batter of 50 g plain flour, 1 egg and seasonings to taste. Mix in 250 g vegetable julienne. Add spoonfuls to hot, shallow oil in a non-stick pan.

2 Fry the fritters over a moderate heat turning once with a spatula until they are crisp and golden on both sides, 3–4 minutes. Drain thoroughly before serving.

STIR-FRYING

This Asian technique is excellent for vegetables, leaving them crisp, full of nutrients and bright in colour. For best results, cut vegetables into julienne or ribbons (see pages 14–15).

Put prepared firm vegetables (here carrots and mangetouts) in a little hot oil in wok. Toss over a high heat for 2 minutes, then add soft vegetables such as bean sprouts and toss for 1 minute. Add seasonings and serve immediately.

DEEP-FRYING POTATOES

The French way of deep-frying potatoes is to "twice-fry" them, which gives an ultra-crisp result. First they are cooked until tender, then they are left to cool, and then they are fried again at a higher temperature. For different shapes, see page 17. Potato baskets are used in classic French cuisine as containers for diced and tiny vegetables; the bird's nest mould for making them is available at specialist kitchenware shops.

1 Heat the oil to 160°C. Immerse potatoes in the oil for 5–6 minutes. Remove and cool, then increase the oil temperature to 180°C and deep-fry the potatoes again until crisp, 1–2 minutes.

2 Lift the basket out of the oil and let as much oil as possible drain away. Empty the fries out of the basket on to paper towels to absorb any residual oil. Sprinkle with salt before serving.

POTATO BASKET
Press *pommes pailles* (see page 17) into bird's nest mould. Deep-fry in 180°C oil for about 3 minutes until crisp and golden. Drain and unmould.

CHARGRILLING

This technique makes use of a stovetop grill to fry vegetables so that they have an attractive striped "chargrilled" effect.

MAKING CRISPY SEAWEED

Although served as seaweed, this Chinese restaurant speciality is in fact a dish of finely shredded spring greens deep-fried until crisp. Remove the tough stalks and wash and dry the leaves before shredding. The drier the cabbage, the easier it is to achieve crispy "seaweed" without it losing its bright green colour.

1 Pour enough oil into a wok to come one-third of the way up the side and heat to 180°C. Reduce the heat slightly, then add shredded greens in batches. Stir constantly with chopsticks to keep the shreds separate.

2 Just at the point the shreds begin to make a tinkling sound, remove with a slotted spoon and drain thoroughly. Serve hot, sprinkled with salt and sugar to taste. If you like, you can also sprinkle the seaweed with the special Chinese seasoning, ground fried fish, as illustrated here.

Cut vegetables (here fennel, courgette, aubergine and red pepper) into chunks and toss them in olive oil, lemon juice, chopped fresh herbs and seasonings. Heat pan until hot but not smoking. Place vegetables on the pan and cook for 5 minutes on each side or until tender.

VEGETABLE MASH & MOULDS

Softened, cooked vegetables are popular accompaniments to meat, poultry and fish, offering contrast in colour and texture. They can be pressed into a smooth or coarse purée or taken one stage further by being shaped in timbale moulds and baked.

MAKING PUREES AND MASH

A food processor or blender can be used for puréeing leafy vegetables (see below). For cooked root vegetables, such as carrots, you can use a machine, but sieving after mashing gives a finer texture. For the smoothest, fluffiest mashed potatoes, use a drum sieve, which has a very fine mesh, or a Mouli, which sieves the potatoes at the same time as puréeing them. Never purée potatoes in a food processor or blender – they may turn gluey.

DRUM SIEVE
Hold sieve secure over a bowl and firmly press cooked vegetables through the mesh with a plastic scraper.

MOULI
Place cooked potatoes in Mouli set over a bowl; turn the crank to force potatoes through into bowl.

MAKING TIMBALES

Puréed vegetables make attractive single servings when cooked in small moulds and turned out upside-down. Spinach is used here, but you can use carrots, broccoli or peas, all of which should be boiled before puréeing (you will need 170 g cooked purée). If you like, you can line the moulds with blanched spinach leaves.

1 Cook 300 g spinach (see left). Purée in a blender with 3 eggs, 250 ml double cream, nutmeg and seasoning. Pour into four buttered 150-ml timbale moulds.

2 Put the timbale moulds in a *bain marie* and bake at 190°C for 20-25 minutes or until firm. Insert a skewer in the centre of a timbale – it should come out clean.

3 Remove the moulds from the *bain marie* and run a knife around the insides to loosen the timbales. Invert on to serving plates and gently lift off the moulds.

MASH

For the best mashed potatoes you need to select the right type of floury potato (see page 17). Once mash is made, choose from the following – all variations on a similar theme – to create a smooth, creamy mash. Season to taste with salt and freshly ground pepper before serving.

- Hot milk and a generous amount of unsalted butter; cream can also be added.
- Crème fraîche and olive oil.
- Olive oil and crushed garlic.
- Hot creamy milk or cream and roasted garlic flesh (see page 36).
- Cream or creamy milk, unsalted butter and grated Gruyère cheese.

COOKING SPINACH

Wash spinach thoroughly, remove and discard the tough stalks and tear the leaves. Although spinach can be cooked in lots of boiling water, to retain its vitamins, minerals and colour, it is far better to steam it (see page 33). Other good methods are to cook it in only the water that clings to the leaves after washing, or to sauté it in olive oil – both methods will take just 2 minutes.

PUREED SOUPS

Puréeing ingredients that have been cooked in stock, water or milk and then enriching the purée with cream or eggs or both is a simple method of making soup. It can be applied to almost any combination of ingredients, even fruit, and is a useful way of using up leftover vegetables.

MAKING PUREED VEGETABLE SOUPS

These are made with one vegetable, such as the carrots here, or with several. Leeks or onions are usually added for flavour. The technique is to cook the vegetables until very soft for easy puréeing. For enriching after puréeing, see opposite page.

1 Sweat diced vegetables in butter over a moderate heat, stirring frequently, for 3–4 minutes until they soften.

2 Add stock or water to cover, and seasonings to taste. Simmer until very soft, about 20 minutes.

3 Purée in a blender, then reheat in a clean pan. Check both the seasonings and the consistency.

FRUIT SOUPS

The puréeing method is ideal for fruit soups. Replace the stock with wine or fruit juices. Pair complementary fruits enhanced with fresh herbs or spices to make refreshing summer soups to serve chilled. Try the following:

- Sour cherry and nectarine.
- Raspberry, strawberry, cinnamon and nectarine.
- Strawberry and rhubarb.
- Melon, mango and basil.
- Apple, pear and cinnamon.
- White peach, apricot and cardamom.
- Papaya, peach and mint.

ALTERNATIVE METHODS OF PUREEING

Vegetable mixtures can be puréed in a number of ways depending on the ingredients they contain. Stringy vegetables, such as green beans and celery, and those with coarse skins like peppers and broad beans, need to be blended and sieved after cooking but before adding stock.

FOOD PROCESSOR
Can be used as an alternative to a blender, but softened vegetables must be puréed without liquid in order to prevent splashing.

HAND BLENDER
For blending small amounts of soup quickly. For hot soups, blend in the pan; for cold soups, decant into a large bowl.

FOOD MILL
Good for coarse-textured vegetables because the fibres are left behind in the mill. Drain vegetables from cooking liquid before milling.

FINE SIEVE
Essential for vegetables with skins such as the roasted yellow peppers shown here. Rub flesh through sieve, then discard skins from sieve.

EAST-WEST FLAVOURS

Certain herbs, spices and condiments characterize particular cuisines. For example, pesto is pure Italian, ginger suggests the Orient, and mint is popular in the Middle East. Contemporary chefs recognize few boundaries these days, and fuse ingredients from both East and West.

CURRY MIXTURES

Although the term curry is often applied to a single spice, it actually refers to a mixture of seasonings. Curry is most famous for its role in Indian cooking, but different powders and pastes are used in many other Asian cuisines.

Indian curry powders, called masalas, are sultry mixtures of native spices, They typically include pepper, cardamom, cinnamon, cumin and coriander (see opposite page).

Thai dishes are characterized by fiery curry blends. Pastes of garlic, lemon grass, chillies, galangal, shrimp paste, fish sauce, coriander and lime zest are common. The green curry paste shown below uses fresh green chillies, while the red uses fiery hot dried red bird's eye chillies.

Chinese curry powder is a mild mix, relying on cinnamon, fennel and coriander seeds, star anise, Sichuan pepper, turmeric and ginger. A small quantity of chilli powder can be included.

PREPARING GINGER

Fresh root ginger is used in many Asian dishes to impart a spicy, mildly hot flavour. Choose plump pieces with smooth, firm skin. The pale yellow flesh is slightly fibrous. To preserve freshness, only peel off the skin covering the flesh to be immediately used. Peeled ginger can be sliced, chopped, grated or crushed.

REMOVING THE SKIN
Use the sharp, heavy blade of a cleaver to scrape away the tough outer skin.

GRATING THE FLESH
A wooden Japanese grater or *oroshigane* is authentic, but a metal box grater will do.

PREPARING THAI FLAVOURINGS

These ingredients offer the intense aromatic flavours that characterize Thai cuisine. Lemon grass, coriander and galingal can be found fresh in most supermarkets. Tamarind can be bought as pods, blocks or concentrate. The latter is most convenient. If bought as pods, the flesh is removed and soaked, to make sour tamarind water.

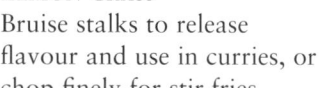

LEMON GRASS
Bruise stalks to release flavour and use in curries, or chop finely for stir-fries.

CORIANDER STEMS
Trim stems and roots; chop finely. Use in curries for pungent flavour.

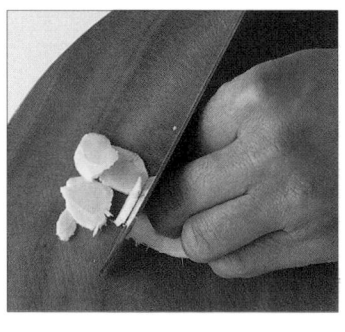

GALINGAL
Like ginger but hotter and more peppery, galingal is first peeled then sliced.

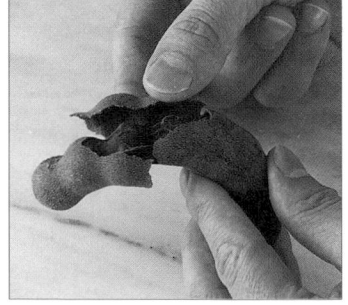

TAMARIND
Remove pulp from pods; soak pulp in hot water 30 minutes, then strain. Use liquid.

GREEN CURRY PASTE

RED CURRY PASTE

MAKING GARAM MASALA

Meaning "a warm blend of spices", this spice mixture is traditionally used in north Indian dishes; it has many variations. Dry-roasting before crushing intensifies the flavour.

1 Combine mace, cinnamon, bay leaf, cardamom, cumin, peppercorns and coriander; stir over a low heat until spices darken.

2 When cool, place toasted spices in a mortar and grind with a pestle until powdery. Store in an airtight container.

PREPARING DRIED SEAWEED

Highly nutritious, dried seaweed is widely used in Japanese cuisine. Toasted dried nori can be crumbled over dishes or used as a wrap; wakame is used in soups, salads and stir-fries.

NORI
Toast sheets over a flame or in the oven for a sweet, delicate flavour.

WAKAME
Soak shreds in warm water to reconstitute; drain thoroughly before use.

SOAKING SAFFRON

This golden-hued, expensive spice is sold in thin, wiry threads that require soaking before use if they are to impart colour and flavour.

Place a pinch of threads in a bowl and pour over hot water. Let soak 10 minutes, then strain; use liquid in sauces and curries.

TOASTING SESAME SEEDS

A popular garnish for Chinese dishes, sesame seeds become rich and nutty when dry-fried. An authentic wok and chopsticks are used here, but a frying pan and wooden spoon can be used instead.

Heat a wok until hot but not smoking, add a handful of sesame seeds and dry-fry over a low heat until golden brown, stirring constantly with chopsticks.

A SELECTION OF ASIAN SPICES AND SEEDS

ASIAN CONDIMENTS

These highly flavoured ingredients are as essential as curry paste in Asian cuisine.

CHINESE FIVE-SPICE POWDER: A fragrant, finely ground blend of star anise, fennel seeds, fagara, cassia and cloves. Used throughout China and Vietnam, usually on roast meat and poultry and in marinades.

JAPANESE SEVEN-SPICE POWDER: A mix of sansho (Japanese pepper), seaweed, chilli, orange zest, poppy seeds and white and black sesame seeds. This mixture is most commonly sprinkled over noodles and soups.

WASABI: A hot flavouring generally served with sushi or sashimi or combined with mayonnaise-based dressings and sauces. Can be grated fresh from horseradish root or prepared from a powder mixed with water.

HERB BUNDLES

The most well-known herb mixture is the bouquet garni (see page 185). This classic combination of thyme, bay, parsley and celery is encompassed in a leek leaf and used to flavour a wide variety of dishes. Here are some suggestions for bouquets garnis to use with specific foods.

BEEF: Pared orange zest, rosemary, thyme and parsley.

FISH AND SHELLFISH: Tarragon, dill and pared lemon zest.

LAMB: Sprigs of rosemary, thyme, savory, mint and parsley.

PORK: Sprigs of fresh sage, thyme and marjoram.

POULTRY: Celery stick with a sprig each of parsley, thyme, marjoram, tarragon and a bay leaf. With game birds, add 6 juniper berries and secure in a muslin bag.

VEGETABLE DISHES AND PULSES: Bay leaf, savory, sage, marjoram, oregano and parsley.

HERB MIXTURES

Western chefs traditionally use specific herb combinations to flavour certain dishes. French dishes are often perfumed with herbes de Provence *and* persillade, *while Italian specialities such as* osso buco *are served with pungent* gremolada.

CHOPPING LEMON ZEST FOR GREMOLADA
Rock the curved blade of a *mezzaluna* over pared strips of lemon zest.

HERBES DE PROVENCE
A mixture of fresh or dried aromatic herbs consisting of thyme, rosemary, bay, basil, savory and even lavender. Delicious as a seasoning for roast lamb and pork.

GREMOLADA
A flavouring from Milan, usually made with finely chopped lemon zest, garlic and parsley. Add at the end of cooking to *osso buco* and other Italian stews.

PERSILLADE
A mixture of chopped parsley and garlic, usually added to dishes just before the end of cooking. It is also combined with fresh breadcrumbs for stuffings.

MAKING PESTO

For enough pesto to serve with 250 g pasta, use 60 g fresh basil, 4 tbsp each extra-virgin olive oil and freshly grated Parmesan cheese, 2–4 garlic cloves, and 30 g pine nuts. Make small quantities by hand, large quantities by machine.

BY HAND

Grind the basil, cheese, garlic and pine nuts in a pestle and mortar. Add the oil gradually to form a granular paste.

BY MACHINE

Work basil, nuts, cheese and garlic with half the oil in a food processor; slowly add remaining oil.

MAKING A TOMATO SAUCE

A quick-cooking tomato sauce is indispensable – not only can it can be used on pizza and pasta, vegetables and meat, but it also forms the base of many classic European dishes. Here fresh plum tomatoes are used; in winter, use canned Italian plum tomatoes.

1 Sweat finely chopped garlic, onion and carrot in olive oil over a moderate heat, 5–7 minutes.

2 Add chopped ripe tomatoes, a little sugar and salt and pepper. Cook until soft, 10–15 minutes.

3 Check seasoning. Use sauce as it is – or, to remove skins and seeds, work through a sieve to a *coulis* consistency.

SPICE MIXTURES

These traditional aromatic blends are greatly favoured by European cooks, who use them to flavour meat and poultry dishes, as well as cakes, biscuits and puddings. The old-fashioned English pickling spice mixture is used in vinegars and a variety of condiments.

GRINDING SPICES
Electric spice or coffee grinders quickly work whole spices to a fine powder.

MIXED SPICE
Also known as pudding spice. Finely grind 1 tbsp coriander seeds, 1 tsp each allspice berries and cloves, and 1 cinnamon stick; mix with 1 tbsp grated nutmeg and 2 tsp ground ginger.

PICKLING SPICE
Combine 2 tbsp ground ginger with 1 tbsp each black peppercorns, white mustard seeds, dried red chillies, allspice berries, dill seed and crushed mace. Add 1 cinnamon stick, crushed, 2 bay leaves, crushed, and 1 tsp whole cloves.

QUATRE-EPICES
A mix of four spices. Combine 1 tbsp black peppercorns, 2 tsp each whole cloves and grated nutmeg and 1 tsp ground ginger. Variations may use allspice and cinnamon.

MIXED SPICE   **PICKLING SPICE**   **QUATRE-EPICES**

VANILLA

Both the pod and seeds of the vanilla bean can be used as flavourings; the seeds impart a stronger flavour than the pod.

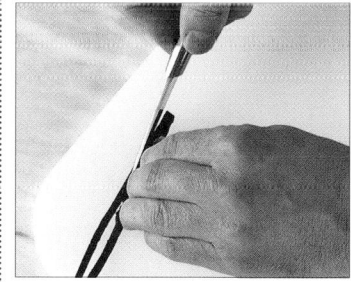

SPLITTING THE POD
Halve pod lengthwise; infuse in warm milk, 30 minutes, or bury in jar of caster sugar.

REMOVING THE SEEDS
Scrape out seeds from halved bean with tip of knife; use as for pod above.

USING HERBS & SPICES

An invaluable addition to the kitchen, fresh herbs and aromatic spices give dishes distinctive taste and ethnic personality. These charts help pair flavourings with the foods they best enhance.

STORING HERBS

Because they do not keep well, fresh herbs are best used straight after picking. The following methods of storage will help keep them fresh and prolong their life, essential techniques in the summer months if you have a herb garden.

• For short storage of 1-2 days, pack freshly picked herbs in plastic bags in the refrigerator. Delicate varieties, such as basil, benefit from being wrapped in slightly damp paper towels before they are placed in bags.

• To dry herbs, hang them up by their stalks in a dry, well-ventilated room. This position concentrates the flavour in the leaves. Once dried, store herbs in airtight containers.

• Fresh herbs can be frozen with excellent results. For best flavour, use young herbs picked before the flowering stage. Gather them in the early morning when the dew has dried and the leaves are at their most aromatic. Strip off the leaves and chop them finely (bay, rosemary, sage and thyme should not be chopped, but snipped into small sprigs). Place chopped herbs in ice-cube trays, cover with iced water and freeze. When solid, pack herb ice cubes in freezer bags, ready to drop into liquids straight from the freezer. Sprigs of herbs should be frozen as they are, in airtight containers.

HERBS AND THEIR USES

	FLAVOUR	USE WITH
BASIL	Sweet, warm, softly spicy, aromatic	White fish, veal, chicken, seafood, salad greens, eggs, tomatoes, pesto and other pasta sauces
BAY	Aromatic, pungent	Soups, stocks, stews, casseroles, sauces (especially béchamel)
CHERVIL	Delicate, slightly anise-like	Fish, chicken, omelettes, sauces
CHIVES	Mild, oniony	Fish, eggs, cheese, salads, creamy soups, potatoes
CORIANDER	Intensely aromatic, spicy	Asian, Middle Eastern and Mexican dishes, carrots, salads, yogurt
CURRY LEAVES	Spicy "curry" flavour	Indian curries, casseroles, soups, seafood, stuffings
DILL	Delicate, anise-like	Salmon, soused herring, veal, carrots, cucumbers, potatoes, mayonnaise, soured cream, soft fresh cheeses
FENNEL	Anise-like	Fish soups, pork, seafood, eggs
MARJORAM/ OREGANO	Sweet, aromatic, pungent	Grilled meats, chicken, tomato sauces, eggs. cheese, flavoured oils and marinades
MINT	Strong, sweet, clean	Cucumber, potatoes, peas, cheese, melon, chilled soups, lamb, yogurt
PARSLEY	Fresh, slightly spicy	Eggs, fish, soups, poultry, meat
ROSEMARY	Pungent, oily, aromatic	Lamb, chicken, pork, bread, potatoes
SAGE	Aromatic, slightly bitter	Pork, veal, duck, goose, turkey, pulses, eggs, ricotta, Parmesan cheese, risotto, pasta
SUMMER SAVORY	Pungent, lemony	Pulses, broad and French beans, eggs, cheese, grilled meats, tomato sauce
TARRAGON	Aromatic, anise-like, cooling	Chicken, eggs, tomatoes, béarnaise
THYME	Intensely aromatic	Poultry and meat roasts and casseroles, roast potatoes

SPICES AND THEIR USES

	FLAVOUR	FORM	USE WITH
ALLSPICE	*Hints of clove and cinnamon*	Whole berries or ground	Caribbean meat stews, game, lamb, onions, cabbage, spiced vinegar, poached fruits, cakes, breads, and pies
CARAWAY	*Aromatic, strong hints of fennel*	Whole seeds or ground	Meat stews, sausages, cabbage, pork, sauerkraut, breads, cheese, rich fruit cakes
CARDAMOM	*Pungent, lemony*	Pods, loose seeds or ground	Indian and Middle Eastern curries, stews, pickling brines, pastries, cakes, fruit dishes, quick breads
CAYENNE/ CHILLI POWDER	*Spicy, very hot*	Ground	Indian, Mexican, Cajun, Caribbean and Creole dishes, seafood, béarnaise sauce
CINNAMON	*Sweet, warm aromatic*	Sticks or ground	Middle-Eastern dishes, curries, fruit desserts, cakes and breads, milk and rice puddings, chocolate desserts
CLOVES	*Sweet, strong*	Whole buds or ground	Ham and pork, sweet potatoes, pumpkin, spiced cakes, apples and other fruits, stocks
CORIANDER	*Fragrant, lemony*	Whole berries or ground	Indian and Oriental dishes, meat, chicken, pickled fish, mushrooms, breads, cakes, pastries and custards
CUMIN	*Pungent, warm, earthy*	Whole seeds or ground	Indian and Mexican dishes, pork, chicken, lamb, cheese, bean soups, rice pilafs
FENNEL SEED		Sweet, liquorice-flavoured	Mediterranean fish soups and stews, grilled fish
GINGER	*Pungent, spicy*	Fresh root or ground	Oriental and Indian dishes, chicken, vegetables, particularly pumpkin and carrots, fruits such as melon and rhubarb, cakes and biscuits
JUNIPER	*Pungent, clean, pine-scented*	Berries	Sausage, pork and game dishes, pâtés and terrines, particularly venison, cabbage, stuffings
MACE	*Sweet, fragrant*	Whole blades or ground	As for nutmeg
MUSTARD	*Pungent, hot*	Whole seeds or ground	Beef and pork, chicken, rabbit, vegetables, pickles and relishes, sauces and dressings
NUTMEG	*Sweet, fragrant*	Whole or ground	Stuffed pastas, meat and béchamel sauces, spinach and potato gratins, cakes and biscuits, milk puddings and custards, mulled wine
PAPRIKA	*Pungent, sweet or hot*	Ground	Meat and poultry, especially Eastern European dishes, eggs, vegetables, cream cheese
PEPPER	*Pungent, mild or hot*	Berries (peppercorns) or ground	Almost every savoury dish and a few sweet ones, such as strawberries and sorbets
POPPY SEEDS	*Nutty, sweet*	Whole and ground	Breads, cakes, pastries, salads, coleslaws, egg noodles, sauces for meat and fish
STAR ANISE	*Warm, aromatic, spicy-sweet*	Whole, broken, seeds and ground	Oriental-style dishes, especially Chinese, pork, duck and chicken, fish and shellfish dishes, marinades
TURMERIC	*Warm, mild aroma*	Whole and ground	Adds subtle flavouring and a distinctive yellow colour, used in curry powders, rice, pulse dishes and chutneys

INDEX